# LAW OFFICE TRANSCRIPTION

# LAW OFFICE TRANSCRIPTION

## Debra A. Differding

Interstate Business College
Fargo, ND


## Sandra Halsne

Interstate Business College
Fargo, ND

KK42AB
PUBLISHED BY
SOUTH-WESTERN PUBLISHING CO.
CINCINNATI, OH                                      DALLAS, TX

Acquisitions Editor: Betty B. Schechter
Editorial Production Manager: Linda R. Allen
Production Editor: Suzanne Dorsey
Designer: James DeSollar
Production Artist: Sophia Renieris
Cover Photo: Stock Photos, Inc./Jeff Spielman

**Library of Congress Cataloging-in-Publication Data**

Differding, Debra A.
    Law office transcription / Debra A. Differding, Sandra Halsne.
        p.       cm.
    Includes index.
    ISBN 0-538-70550-7
    1. Legal secretaries—United States—Handbooks, manuals, etc.
2. Dictation (Office practice)       I. Halsne, Sandra.
II. Title.
KF319.D54   1992
347.73'504—dc20
[347.307504]                                                    91-27144
                                                                        CIP

# PREFACE

Proficiency in producing mailable copy directly from a dictation tape is a top-priority skill in today's law offices. Secretarial graduates who (1) are familiar with the basic areas of the law and with the legal proceedings specific to each discipline and who (2) possess the skills necessary to transcribe mailable and correctly formatted copy will compete more favorably for today's legal secretarial positions.

**OBJECTIVES**

*Law Office Transcription* is a text-workbook designed to teach legal secretarial students how to use a transcribing machine and how to format legal correspondence and legal documents directly from a dictation tape into mailable form. This text-workbook would also be effective for in-service training or as cross training for legal secretaries.

In *Law Office Transcription*, students will produce correspondence and documents from actual legal cases, thus familiarizing them with many of the basic areas of the law and with the legal papers specific to each discipline. In addition, students will learn specialized rules of punctuation, Latin terms, and standards for preparing legal documents.

Upon completion of this course, the legal secretarial student should be able to

- Define given legal terminology.
- Operate a transcribing machine efficiently.
- Proofread accurately.
- Apply rules of spelling, grammar, and punctuation.
- Use reference materials effectively.
- Key mailable materials directly from dictation tapes.

**ORGANIZATION**

*Law Office Transcription* is divided into ten legal cases, each relating to a different area of the law. Each case has been researched from actual law office files. Students will work on each case from its onset through its conclusion, formatting a variety of documents and correspondence.

Each case is complete in itself. It includes background information about the legal action, terminology particular to that type of action, and commonly transcribed documents and correspondence. This course may be tailored to the number of course hours available. The sequence of the cases may also be altered because there is minimal variation in the degree of difficulty among cases.

**CASE STUDIES**

*Law Office Transcription* is comprised of ten case studies:

CASE 1.   Mechanic's Lien
CASE 2.   Credit, Collection, and Default Judgment
CASE 3.   Legal Potpourri
CASE 4.   Change of Venue
CASE 5.   Wills and Probate

CASE  6.   Personal Injury Litigation
CASE  7.   Rescission and Revocation of Contract
CASE  8.   Corporate
CASE  9.   Dissolution of Marriage
CASE 10.   Mortgage Foreclosure

**STUDENT TEXT-WORKBOOK**

In order to become familiar with the background of a project, students study a case instruction sheet and a terminology list relating to each case before transcription begins. These instruction sheets include the case name, the names of the parties involved in the action, the names of their attorneys, the venue for the action, the number of jobs contained in the case, a brief description of each job, and a list of legal terms common to the action. Students are expected to supply most punctuation, to use acceptable formats for documents and correspondence, to employ appropriate preprinted forms, and to produce mailable copy directly from dictation tapes.

A reference section of rules and guidelines for formatting business letters, memos, and court and noncourt documents, a glossary of Latin words and phrases, and general rules for keyboarding land descriptions in real estate papers is included in the text-workbook. Also included are model documents that illustrate the content and format of correctly prepared legal papers. Letterheads, memo forms, legal cap, and other preprinted forms are included with each case.

**INSTRUCTOR'S MANUAL**

A comprehensive *Instructor's Manual* is available that discusses the design of the course, suggestions for teaching the course, production standards, and grading procedures. The manual also contains a test bank. The test bank includes a written quiz and a transcription production test for each of the ten cases. All case solutions as well as solutions to the written quizzes and the production tests are provided in the *Instructor's Manual.* Model documents that may be used as transparency masters for classroom instruction are provided as well.

**AUDIOCASSETTES**

The ten legal cases in *Law Office Transcription* are dictated on cassettes to be transcribed by the student. These cassettes are dictated at various speeds, with some cassettes employing the use of office-style dictation. Several different regional accents are used in the recorded dictation.

**ACKNOWLEDGMENTS**

The authors gratefully acknowledge the following who gave their time, support, and encouragement during the preparation of this text:

The Administration of Interstate
  Business College
Fargo, ND

Lydia M. Nofil, Lecturer
New York City Technical College
New York City, NY

Garaas Law Firm
Fargo, ND

Cahill & Maring, PA
Moorhead, MN

Nilles, Hansen & Davies, Ltd.
Fargo, ND

Linnerooth Law Firm
Fargo, ND

Gunhus, Grinnell, Klinger,
  Swenson & Guy
Moorhead, MN

# CONTENTS

# INTRODUCTION

stefansen
cohen &
skramstad

**WELCOME TO STEFANSEN, COHEN & SKRAMSTAD**

You will be employed as a legal secretary for the firm of
STEFANSEN, COHEN & SKRAMSTAD. This law firm has a main
office located in Fargo, North Dakota, and a satellite
office located in Moorhead, Minnesota. The attorneys in
the firm are the three senior partners, Gail S. Stefansen,
Bernard J. Cohen, and Ann D. Skramstad, and the three
associate attorneys, Tomas J. Lopez, Neil W. Webster, and
Barbara L. Walker. Susan A. Barnes is the Office Administrator in the main office, and Diana B. Perez is the
Office Administrator in the satellite office. Fargo-
Moorhead is a border city community, and the lawyers in
this firm practice law in both states. You will be transcribing legal documents and correspondence relating to
ten different cases for several of the lawyers employed
by the firm. These cases represent actual cases that have
been obtained from law office files. You will be involved
with each case from its onset through its conclusion,
keying various documents and correspondence for the
attorneys of this firm.

Because of the confidential nature of law office files,
you will be asked to read and sign a confidentiality
statement prior to beginning your duties.

We look forward to a rewarding working relationship, and
we hope that your employment as a legal secretary at
STEFANSEN, COHEN & SKRAMSTAD will be a valuable experience.

Sincerely

Susan A. Barnes
Diana B. Perez
Office Administrators

**Attorneys at Law**

Gail S. Stefansen, Bernard J. Cohen, Ann D. Skramstad
HOME OFFICE: 3201 Interstate Avenue, Fargo, ND 58103-8773 (701) 555-1294
Neil W. Webster, Barbara L. Walker, Tomas J. Lopez
SATELLITE OFFICE: 2213 Roosevelt Avenue, Moorhead, MN 56560-9909 (218) 555-1781

## CONFIDENTIALITY POLICY

It is common knowledge that the normal operation of a law office exposes confidential professional information to nonlawyers, particularly secretaries and other employees with access to the files. Confidential information and privileged communications are a vital part of the attorney/secretary/client relationship. The importance of preserving confidential and privileged information is an uncompromising obligation of every employee of a law firm.

To ensure the confidentiality of client information, all employees of STEFANSEN, COHEN & SKRAMSTAD must sign a statement acknowledging this confidentiality policy. Any violation of this policy will result in immediate disciplinary action.

## CONFIDENTIALITY STATEMENT

```
I, _____, an employee of
STEFANSEN, COHEN & SKRAMSTAD, have read and reviewed the
confidentiality policy with the Office Administrator. I
understand the importance of this policy for each
employee. I further understand that if I intentionally
violate this policy by any unauthorized release of client
information, this violation will constitute grounds for
my immediate dismissal.



_____          _____
Date                                     Signature of Employee
```

## OBJECTIVES

In *Law Office Transcription*, students learn how to use a transcribing machine and how to prepare legal correspondence and legal documents directly from a dictation tape. Students also become familiar with documents and correspondence common to specific legal proceedings. Objectives of the class are

- To define given legal terminology
- To operate a transcribing machine efficiently
- To proofread accurately
- To apply rules of spelling, grammar, and punctuation
- To use reference materials effectively
- To key mailable materials directly from dictation tapes

In *Law Office Transcription*, students key *actual* legal documents from *actual* legal cases. They follow a legal action from its onset to its conclusion. Students not only become familiar with keying legal documents, they also become familiar with different types of law and with relevant legal terminology.

## LENGTH OF COURSE

There are ten transcription projects in *Law Office Transcription*:

CASE 1. Mechanic's Lien
CASE 2. Credit, Collection, and Default Judgment
CASE 3. Legal Potpourri
CASE 4. Change of Venue
CASE 5. Wills and Probate

CASE  6.  Personal Injury Litigation
CASE  7.  Rescission and Revocation of Contract
CASE  8.  Corporate
CASE  9.  Dissolution of Marriage
CASE 10.  Mortgage Foreclosure

Before beginning a transcription project, students study a case instruction sheet and a list of legal terms for each case. The instruction sheet and the legal terminology provide the background for the upcoming project. Relevant background information includes the case name, the names of the parties involved in the action, the names of their attorneys, the venue for the action, the number and type of jobs contained in the case, and legal terms common to the case. This information serves as a reference guide for transcribing the case.

Some punctuation is dictated to you, but it is the secretary's responsibility to supply most punctuation. All materials must be completed in proper legal format, and they must meet standards of mailability. Use preprinted forms as instructed.

**EVALUATIONS**

Upon completion of each case, you are required to (1) take a written quiz that will cover legal terminology, background information, and general information regarding the materials keyed; and (2) transcribe a taped production test, which consists of one document relating to the case just completed, directly into mailable form (to be graded by your instructor).

**REFERENCES AND ILLUSTRATIONS**

The reference section contains rules and guidelines for keying business letters, interoffice memos, and court and noncourt documents. Several illustrations are included to aid in your transcription of documents. Be aware that legal forms and documents vary from state to state. The formatting of these forms and documents may also vary from law office to law office. Check the format used in your office by reviewing other files or office manuals. It is important to remember to be consistent!

The ability to transcribe with speed, accuracy, and neatness is vital if a transcriptionist is to be an asset to a law office. A broad vocabulary, good spelling and grammar, and knowledge of legal forms and document formatting are necessary, although much of the latter is learned in individual law offices to conform to individual standards.

Each document and each case in a law office is unique; therefore, assumptions or guesses should not be made when preparing legal material. Rather than make embarrassing or possibly costly errors refer to resource material or ask the Office Administrator or an attorney if you are unsure about something.

Too much emphasis cannot be placed upon the need for using resource material to find the correct answer to a question. If in doubt about the spelling or the definition of a word, refer to a good dictionary. For questions about the meaning of legal terms or Latin words and phrases, use a law dictionary. The libraries in most law firms include almanacs and encyclopedias, which contain general and statistical information, and biographical and gazetteer indices of good dictionaries, which identify persons and places. The telephone directory, too, can often be helpful. Many offices have handbooks or manuals that contain detailed instructions regarding office standards for formatting documents and letters.

# TRANSCRIBING CORRESPONDENCE AND LEGAL DOCUMENTS

**BUSINESS LETTERS**

| LETTER STYLES | DESCRIPTION |
| --- | --- |
| Block | Dateline and complimentary closing begin at the left margin; all other lines begin at the left margin. |
| Modified Block | Dateline and complimentary closing begin at center; all other lines begin at the left margin. Paragraphs may or may not be indented. |

The steps in keying a business letter are as follows (refer the sample letter depicted in Figure 1):

1. Set proper margins for the length of the letter; set tab stops where needed. Side margins should be set for a 6-inch line (60 pica spaces/ 72 elite spaces).
2. Key the dateline on line 13 or line 16. (Placement of the dateline may vary with the length of letter.)
3. Key the letter address a quadruple space (QS) below the dateline.
4. Key the salutation a double space (DS) below the letter address.
5. DS and key the reference line. The location of the reference line may differ from one law firm to another. Check the sample letter (Figure 1) for the preferred format for STEFANSEN, COHEN & SKRAMSTAD.

   All letters should include a reference line whether it is dictated or not. It is generally the secretary's responsibility to supply the proper reference line for all letters.
6. DS and begin keying the body of the letter; DS between paragraphs.
7. DS and key the complimentary close.
8. Key the name of the attorney handling the matter on the fourth line below the complimentary close. If the law firm's name is used in the closing, it is keyed in solid caps a DS below the complimentary closing. The name of the attorney signing the letter is then keyed on the fourth line below the firm's name.
9. Key the dictator's initials and the keyboard operator's initials, called reference initials, a DS below the signature line.

   Often a legal assistant is asked to write a letter for an attorney's signature; consequently, the person who signs the letter is not always the person who composes it. In this case, the composer's initials and the keyboard operator's initials are used.

10. Enclosure notations are keyed a DS below the reference initials.
11. Copy notations are keyed a DS below the enclosure notation.
12. Postscripts are keyed a DS below the last notation on the letter.

Remember, it is the responsibility of the secretary to supply most punctuation; however, some punctuation is dictated on the *Law Office Transcription* audiocassettes. It is also the secretary's responsibility to make sure that all addresses include a ZIP Code. If the ZIP Code is not dictated to you nor provided in the case instruction sheet, look it up in a ZIP Code directory.

## Two-Letter State Abbreviations

| STATE ABBREVIATIONS RECOMMENDED BY THE U.S. POST OFFICE | | | |
|---|---|---|---|
| Alabama | AL | Montana | MT |
| Alaska | AK | Nebraska | NE |
| Arizona | AZ | Nevada | NV |
| Arkansas | AR | New Hampshire | NH |
| California | CA | New Jersey | NJ |
| Colorado | CO | New Mexico | NM |
| Connecticut | CT | New York | NY |
| Delaware | DE | North Carolina | NC |
| District of Columbia | DC | North Dakota | ND |
| Florida | FL | Ohio | OH |
| Georgia | GA | Oklahoma | OK |
| Hawaii | HI | Oregon | OR |
| Idaho | ID | Pennsylvania | PA |
| Illinois | IL | Puerto Rico | PR |
| Indiana | IN | Rhode Island | RI |
| Iowa | IA | South Carolina | SC |
| Kansas | KS | South Dakota | SD |
| Kentucky | KY | Tennessee | TN |
| Louisiana | LA | Texas | TX |
| Maine | ME | Utah | UT |
| Maryland | MD | Vermont | VT |
| Massachusetts | MA | Virginia | VA |
| Michigan | MI | Washington | WA |
| Minnesota | MN | West Virginia | WV |
| Mississippi | MS | Wisconsin | WI |
| Missouri | MO | Wyoming | WY |

**FIGURE 1**
Sample Business Letter, Block Style

stefansen
cohen &
skramstad

September 1, 19xx ◄— **ABOUT LINE 13**

Mr. Robert C. Blakewell ◄— **LETTER ADDRESS**
19234 Center Parkway
Moorhead, MN  56560-4567

Dear Mr. Blakewell ◄— **SALUTATION**

Re:  Lynwood vs. Washington et al. ◄— **REFERENCE LINE**
     Our File:  SGH99-1003
     Your File:  RCB8999-9

I have now had an opportunity to review this matter with Ms. Langeloh
and enclose a copy of her letter for your information.  She has
indicated that if your client will pay her the sum of $4,950.95, the
matter can be settled.  You would not then have to interpose an answer
or proceed any further in this matter.

If this does not meet with your client's approval, I would suggest that
you serve an answer so that we can notify the Court and set the matter
for trial.

Yours very truly ◄— **COMPLIMENTARY CLOSE**

Barbara L. Walker ◄— **SIGNATURE LINE**

BLW/sh ◄— **REFERENCE INITIALS**

Enclosure ◄— **ENCLOSURE NOTATION**

c Ms. Heidi J. Langeloh ◄— **COPY NOTATION**

This is an example of a postscript.  A postscript is a short note
appended to the end of a letter.

POSTSCRIPT

**Attorneys at Law**
Gall S. Stefansen, Bernard J. Cohen, Ann D. Skramstad
HOME OFFICE: 3201 Interstate Avenue, Fargo, ND  58103-8773 (701) 555-1294

Nell W. Webster, Barbara L. Walker, Tomas J. Lopez
SATELLITE OFFICE: 2213 Roosevelt Avenue, Moorhead, MN  56560-9909 (218) 555-1781

**WHAT MAKES A LETTER UNMAILABLE?**

1. Misspelled word
2. Word divided incorrectly at the end of a line
3. Typographical error
4. Transposition of words
5. Letter too high on page
6. Letter too low on page
7. Letter too far to the right of the page
8. Letter too far to the left of the page
9. Messy erasure or hole in paper
10. Material omitted or changed that obviously alters the meaning of the letter
11. Omission of the dateline
12. Omission of enclosure notation when needed
13. Omission of title (Dr., Mr., Mrs., Ms.) in the letter address or salutation
14. Abbreviated compass direction in the letter address (N for North)
15. Abbreviated type of thoroughfare (St. for Street)
16. Right margin too ragged or uneven—more than 6 spaces between the longest line and shortest line of the body (a short line at the end of a paragraph is acceptable)
17. Omission of a comma between two independent clauses joined by a conjunction
18. Omission of a comma after an introductory clause (beginning with *if, when,* etc.)
19. Omission of a comma between words in a series
20. Omission of an apostrophe to show possession

**INTEROFFICE MEMOS**

The steps in typing an interoffice memo are as follows (refer to the sample memo depicted in Figure 2):

1. Key the appropriate information after each guide word. Make sure that the words following *TO, FROM, DATE,* and *SUBJECT* align at the left.
2. Begin keying the message a triple space (TS) below the last guide word line.
3. Single-space (SS) the body of the memo. Paragraphs may be blocked or indented, depending on office standards. Block style is the preferred style for memos at STEFANSEN, COHEN & SKRAMSTAD.
4. The dictator's initials may be keyed in capital letters a DS below the body of the memo at center.
5. Key reference initials a DS below the dictator's initials, if the dictator's initials are used, or a DS below the body of the memo at the left margin.
6. Enclosure notations, attachment notations, and copy notations follow the reference initials as in a letter.
7. Memos are not signed but may be initialed by the dictator at the top of the memo next to his or her name.

Transcribing Correspondence and Legal Documents

**FIGURE 2**
Sample Memo

stefansen, cohen & skramstad

# Interoffice Memo

TO:   All Legal Transcription       DATE:   January 12, 19xx
      Students

FROM:   Susan A. Barnes         SUBJECT:  Keying Memos
      Office Administrator

The information displayed in this sample memo is to serve
as your guide for keying interoffice memorandums.

Follow each step carefully, checking your work against this
sample.  Feel free to ask questions.

                             SAB

sh

**Attorneys at Law**
**Gail S. Stefansen, Bernard J. Cohen, Ann D. Skramstad**
HOME OFFICE: 3201 Interstate Avenue, Fargo, ND  58103-8773 (701) 555-1294

**Neil W. Webster, Barbara L. Walker, Tomas J. Lopez**
SATELLITE OFFICE: 2213 Roosevelt Avenue, Moorhead, MN  56560-9909 (218) 555-1781

A competent legal secretary understands the content of legal documents. If you understand the content of a legal document, you will be able to catch errors in grammar and content. For example, if the attorney dictates *defendant* when *plaintiff* is intended, you can correct this error.

*PROOFREAD EVERY PAPER YOU KEY BEFORE REMOVING IT FROM YOUR TYPEWRITER OR SENDING IT TO THE PRINTER.* Accuracy is very important in the legal profession. In fact, lawsuits may result from inaccuracies and careless keyboarding errors.

There are two broad categories of legal documents: court documents and noncourt documents. More information regarding these important classes of documents is provided on pages 16–28.

Legal documents may be keyed on standard-sized typing paper (8½ x 11 inches) or on legal-sized paper (8½ x 13 or 8½ x 14 inches). Many states now have rules governing the size of paper that can be used for legal documents. Legal cap, white paper with ruled margins at left and right, may also be used. All keying on legal cap is done within the ruled margins. Legal cap is commonly used for legal documents in some states and is often used for wills.

The following guidelines offer practical, widely accepted standards for keying legal documents.

## Abbreviations

Do not use abbreviations, such as state abbreviations, in the body of a legal document.

## Acknowledgment Clause

Many noncourt documents must be signed before a notary public. The notary completes the acknowledgment clause, which is either keyed or preprinted at the end of the document, at the time the document is notarized. Susan A. Barnes and Diana B. Perez, Office Administrators at STEFANSEN, COHEN & SKRAMSTAD, are notaries. They are responsible for notarizing all documents keyed at STEFANSEN, COHEN & SKRAMSTAD that require notarization.

## Copies

When preparing legal documents, determine the number of copies to be made as follows: original for the court, a copy for each attorney representing a party to the action, a file copy, and a copy for the client (if this is office practice). Law offices often make *conformed copies* of executed documents for their files and for other parties involved in the matter. To conform a copy, any blanks that were filled in on the original at the time of execution are keyed or handwritten on the copy. Signatures are keyed on the signature lines of the copy preceded by the symbol /s/, and any information that was added to or deleted from the original is also keyed or handwritten on the copy. The copy then becomes an exact duplicate of the original; that is, it becomes a conformed copy.

## Corrections and Additions

Avoid erasures or corrections. Do not alter principal figures, names, places, or dates if the alteration might make a person suspect that the document was changed after it was signed. If additional material must be added to a document after it has been keyed, rekey as many pages as necessary to include such material. Do not key inserts on separate pages. However, a rider with additional material may be attached to preprinted forms such as leases, mortgages, etc.

### Dating Documents

Every legal document should be dated. The date may be keyed in different ways (e.g., Dated this third day of May, 19xx; Dated this 21st day of June, 19xx; Dated: Fargo, North Dakota, November 1, 19xx).

Dates are either provided when dictated or, if the document is not signed or executed immediately, are supplied at some later time. Refer to the sample documents that follow for examples of the style for dating documents preferred by STEFANSEN, COHEN & SKRAMSTAD.

### Hyphenation

The last word on a page or at the end of a paragraph should never be hyphenated. Hyphenation of words should be avoided as much as possible and used only after consulting a dictionary.

### Incomplete Pages

*Always* leave at least two lines of a paragraph on a page and carry at least two lines of a paragraph forward to the next page. Avoid ending a page with a complete sentence, although instances will occur that will make such page breaks impossible. As protection against substitution or addition of pages preceding the signature, signature lines may never appear alone on the last page of any legal document. At least two lines of the document should be carried over to the page that is to be signed. Extra space can be added to the next-to-last page in order to carry two typed lines over to the signature page. A large *Z ruling* is often drawn in the blank space to indicate that extra space has intentionally been added to that page of the document.

### Indentations

The first line of each paragraph may be indented 5 or 10 spaces. At STEFANSEN, COHEN & SKRAMSTAD, paragraphs are indented 5 spaces, unless the dictator designates a different indentation. Any material that is to be set apart from the rest of the text of a document is usually double-indented (10 or 15 spaces left and right) and single-spaced. Again, at STEFANSEN, COHEN & SKRAMSTAD, 10 spaces are used for double indentations, unless the dictator indicates otherwise. Most quotations of 50 or more words are double-indented and single-spaced.

### Introductory and Closing Phrases

Introductory phrases at the beginning of a document and at the beginning of new sections in a document appear in all caps for easy reference and for emphasis. Closing phrases are also keyed in all caps. Capitalization of certain words and phrases is standard:

- THE STATE OF MINNESOTA TO THE ABOVE-NAMED DEFENDANTS
- IN WITNESS WHEREOF
- KNOW ALL MEN BY THESE PRESENTS
- YOU ARE HEREBY SUMMONED
- WHEREFORE

- IT IS HEREBY STIPULATED AND AGREED
- PLEASE TAKE NOTICE
- WHEREAS
- THIS INDENTURE
- THIS AGREEMENT
- NOW, THEREFORE
- RESOLVED

## Document Names and Terms

In the interest of speed and efficiency, many firms, including STEFANSEN, COHEN & SKRAMSTAD, no longer capitalize document names or terms such as *plaintiff, defendant,* etc. However, words that are capitalized in regular, nonlegal documents are also capitalized in legal documents. In addition, in legal documents, other words may *always* be capitalized (e.g., Judge and Justice). When the word *court* refers to a courtroom or an institution dealing with a case, it is not capitalized. When a specific court is referred to by title, such as District Court, it is capitalized. When *court* refers to the judge hearing the case, it is capitalized (e.g., *the Court hereby states* means that the judge is stating). Generally, if you can substitute the word *court* for *judge* and retain the meaning, it is capitalized. Legal offices also generally capitalize these three words: *City, County,* and *State* (e.g., City of Fargo, County of Cass, State of North Dakota). Unless otherwise directed, these words should be capitalized.

Because of the particular formality of wills, the words *Last Will and Testament, Codicil, Personal Representative,* and *Executor* or *Executrix* are always keyed with initial caps. Names of persons cited in a will or codicil are keyed in all caps.

## Capitalization of Venues

In legal documents, the state and county (venue) where the document is executed or where the trial takes place is keyed in all caps.

| *Example:* | STATE OF MINNESOTA |
| | |
| | COUNTY OF CLAY |

If the venue appears a second time in a document (such as on an affidavit), the second venue is keyed in uppercase and lowercase letters.

| *Example:* | State of Minnesota | ) | |
| | | ) ss. |
| | County of Clay | ) | |

## Legal Backs

In some states all legal documents, including court documents, must be placed in a *legal back.* A legal back is a heavy sheet of paper, longer than the document itself, often of colored paper. The extra length of the backing sheet (¾ to 1 inch) is folded over the top of the document. The document is inserted under the fold and stapled into the backing sheet with two staples placed about ½ inch from the top fold. For court documents, the venue, the name of the parties, and the title of the document is keyed on the reverse side of the backing sheet. For noncourt documents, the legal back includes the names of the parties involved, the name of the document, and the date. The name and address of the law firm may be preprinted or keyed on the legal back (see Figure 3). Office file copies are not backed.

**REFERENCE SECTION**

Index No. 24-0862          Year 19 xx

IN DISTRICT COURT
CASS COUNTY, NORTH DAKOTA

Jane Doe,

                    Plaintiff,

    vs.

John Doe,

                    Defendant.

SUMMONS AND COMPLAINT

Ann D. Skramstad
Stefansen, Cohen & Skramstad
*Attorney for* Plaintiff

*Office and Post Office Address, Telephone*

3201 Interstate Avenue
Fargo, ND  58103-8773
(701) 555-1294

To

Attorney(s) for

Service of a copy of the within
                              is hereby admitted.
Dated,

    ------------------------------------------------

Attorney(s) for

---

Juli K. Morgan,

                    Employee

    and

Brown, James & Adams

                    Employer

EMPLOYMENT AGREEMENT

Ann D. Skramstad
Stefansen, Cohen & Skramstad
3201 Interstate Avenue
Fargo, ND  58103-8773
(701) 555-1294

May 5, 19xx

## Margins

Noncourt documents begin with a 2-inch top margin on the first page, using 1½-inch top margins on succeeding pages and 1-inch bottom margins throughout. The side margins begin 2 spaces inside legal cap rulings. If plain paper is used, the side margins should be set for a 6-inch line (60 pica spaces/72 elite spaces).

## Numbers and Money Amounts

Extreme care must be taken in keying numbers and sums of money. In most states, the current trend in handling numbers is to use figures. However, amounts of money are commonly keyed in words and repeated in figures in varying styles. Two commonly used styles for keying money amounts are listed here:

1.  Nine Hundred Twenty-two and 79/100 Dollars ($922.79)
2.  NINE HUNDRED TWENTY-TWO and 79/100 DOLLARS ($922.79)

At STEFANSEN, COHEN & SKRAMSTAD, lists of money amounts are keyed in figures. Sums of money are keyed according to the format enumerated in item (1) above. Some law firms do not use these formats (remember, you must be knowledgeable about your office style).

## Pagination

Center page numbers at the bottom of the page, not less than ½ inch from the bottom. First pages are not numbered.

## Preprinted Forms

When filling in blank spaces on preprinted forms (forms for deeds, mortgages, sales contracts, etc.), be careful to align all copies of the form properly if making carbon copies. If the keyed material does not fill the space allowed for it, draw a line with a black pen from the end of the keyed line to the right margin and from the left margin at the bottom of the blank area straight across the page to the right margin. Join the two horizontal lines with a diagonal line in the form of an enlarged *Z*, called a *Z ruling*. Fill in short spaces keying a row of hyphens. Because of the increasing use of computers in today's legal offices, many preprinted forms are no longer used. They have, however, been converted to computerized forms and are quite commonly used in this manner.

## Rough Drafts

The number and date of each rough draft of a legal document, along with the dictator's and keyboard operator's initials, should be keyed in the upper left margin on the first page. The first draft should be labeled FIRST DRAFT; the second, SECOND DRAFT, as follows:

*Example:*
```
FIRST DRAFT
JUNE 19, 19xx
JCW/sh
```

All drafts should be kept until the document is keyed in its final form.

### Signature Lines

Signature lines are keyed from the center of the page to the right margin, a QS apart to provide ample room for signatures. The signer's name should be keyed, exactly as it appears in the document, a SS below the blank as shown in Figure 4.

If occupational titles are keyed as part of the signature line, they are keyed as shown in the sample signature lines illustrated in Figure 4. Occupational titles are used with the names of company officers (president, vice president, etc.) and with notary publics.

If signature lines for witnesses are to be keyed, follow the format illustrated in Figure 4.

**FIGURE 4**
Sample Signature Lines

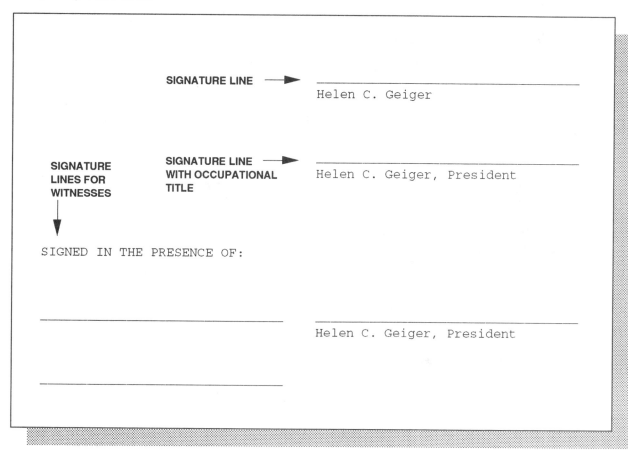

### Spacing

As a general rule, all legal documents and court papers are double-spaced. Some material, such as land descriptions, quotations, and coded information, is single-spaced.

### Titles

Key the title of a noncourt document 2 inches from the top of the first page and center it in all caps. If the title is more than one line, SS between lines in the title. A TS separates the title from the body of the document.

### Verification Clause

It may be necessary in some jurisdictions for the plaintiff to sign a verification stating that the allegations contained in a document are true and correct. Verification clauses must be sworn to before a notary public. Verifications are only used in pleadings (i.e., documents that contain allegations).

## COURT DOCUMENTS

### Caption Format

The caption normally begins on line 10; however, captions may be formatted differently from one office to another. Some states have court rules that regulate the line on which the caption must begin. Figures 5–7 display acceptable caption formats. It is the secretary's responsibility to choose the appropriate caption for the document that is being transcribed by studying the case instruction sheet.

## FIGURE 5
State Court Caption Format, Version 1 (for Minnesota)

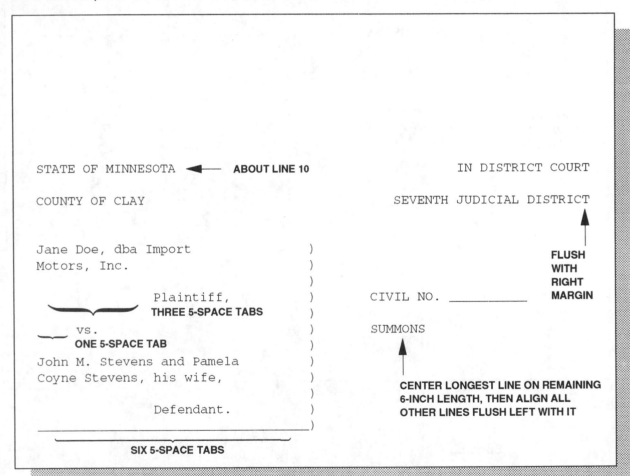

Transcribing Correspondence and Legal Documents

**FIGURE 6**
State Court Caption Format, Version 2 (for North Dakota)

```
          IN DISTRICT COURT, CASS COUNTY, STATE OF NORTH DAKOTA


Jane Doe dba Import                )
Motors, Inc.                       )
                                   )
              Plaintiff,           )     CIVIL NO. _____
                                   )
     vs.                           )     ORDER FOR DEFAULT JUDGMENT
                                   )     ON FAILURE TO ANSWER
John M. Stevens and Pamela         )
Coyne Stevens, his wife,           )
                                   )
              Defendants.          )
_____)
```

**FIGURE 7**
Federal Court Caption Format

```
               IN THE UNITED STATES DISTRICT COURT
             FOR THE SOUTHWESTERN DISTRICT OF MINNESOTA


Jane Doe,                          )
                                   )
              Plaintiff,           )     CIVIL NO. _____
                                   )
     vs.                           )     COMPLAINT
                                   )
John Doe,                          )
                                   )
              Defendant.           )
_____)
```

## Signature Blocks

Figure 8 contains two acceptable formats for signature blocks. The law office of STEFANSEN, COHEN & SKRAMSTAD prefers the first version. The use of license numbers in attorneys' signature blocks is not required in all states.

**FIGURE 8**
Sample Signature Blocks

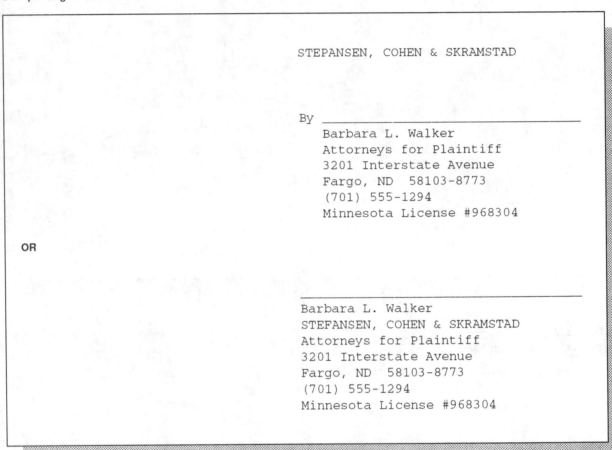

```
                          STEPANSEN, COHEN & SKRAMSTAD




                      By _____
                          Barbara L. Walker
                          Attorneys for Plaintiff
                          3201 Interstate Avenue
                          Fargo, ND  58103-8773
                          (701) 555-1294
                          Minnesota License #968304




                          _____
                          Barbara L. Walker
                          STEFANSEN, COHEN & SKRAMSTAD
                          Attorneys for Plaintiff
                          3201 Interstate Avenue
                          Fargo, ND  58103-8773
                          (701) 555-1294
                          Minnesota License #968304
```

**OR**

After you have examined the preceding caption formats and signature blocks, you should look carefully at all the sample legal documents that appear on pages 19–28.

**FIGURE 9**
Sample Summons

IN DISTRICT COURT, COUNTY OF CASS, STATE OF NORTH DAKOTA

```
Jane Doe,                           )
                                    )
              Plaintiff,            )       CIVIL NO. _____
                                    )
       vs.                          )       SUMMONS
                                    )
John Doe,                           )
                                    )
              Defendant.            )
_____)
```

THE STATE OF NORTH DAKOTA TO THE ABOVE-NAMED DEFENDANTS:

YOU ARE HEREBY SUMMONED and required to appear and defend this complaint, which is herewith served upon you, by serving upon the undersigned an answer or other proper response within twenty (20) days after the service of this summons upon you, exclusive of the day of service.  If you fail to do so, judgment by default will be taken against you for the relief demanded in the complaint.

Dated this _____ day of _____, 19xx.

STEFANSEN, COHEN & SKRAMSTAD

By _____
Ann D. Skramstad
Attorneys for Plaintiff
3201 Interstate Avenue
Fargo, ND  58103-8773
(701) 555-1294
North Dakota License #508777

**FIGURE 10**
Sample Sections from an Employment Agreement

EMPLOYMENT AGREEMENT

As of the 27th day of July, 19xx, CHARLES H. KETCHUM, doing business as KETCHUM AND ASSOCIATES, "EMPLOYER," and ROBERT P. DIAZ, "EMPLOYEE," agree as follows:

I.    EMPLOYMENT.

EMPLOYER employs EMPLOYEE and EMPLOYEE accepts employment upon the terms and conditions of this agreement.

A.   During employment hereunder, EMPLOYEE will have access to confidential information consisting of the following categories of information (collectively, the "Trade Secrets"):

1.   Financial information, such as EMPLOYER'S earnings, assets, and debts;

2.   Supply and service information, such as goods and services.

INTENDING TO BE LEGALLY BOUND, the parties have executed this agreement as of the date first written above.

KETCHUM AND ASSOCIATES


_____

CHARLES H. KETCHUM

(EMPLOYER)


_____

ROBERT P. DIAZ

(EMPLOYEE)

**FIGURE 11**
Sample Exhibit A

REFERENCE SECTION

EXHIBIT A

State of North Dakota     )
                          ) ss.
County of Cass            )


    Helen C. Geiger, being first duly sworn on oath, deposes and states that she is the plaintiff in the foregoing complaint; that she has read the complaint and knows the contents thereof; and that the same is true of her own knowledge, except as to those matters stated on information and belief.

    Your affiant further states that all materials were furnished as alleged in said complaint.

    Dated this _____ day of _____, 19xx.


                              _____
                              Helen C. Geiger

    Subscribed and sworn to before me this _____ day of
_____, 19xx.


                              _____
                              Susan A Barnes, Notary Public
                              Cass County, North Dakota
                              My commission expires:  9-26-96

## Affidavit of Service by Mail

If your office does not provide preprinted forms for affidavits of service by mail, then Figure 12 illustrates a format that is acceptable to most law offices. If you are using word processing equipment, you can store this document as a shell, leaving blanks where information may vary from case to case.

**FIGURE 12**
Sample Affidavit of Service by Mail

```
INSERT APPROPRIATE VENUE

↓

STATE OF MINNESOTA          )
                            ) ss.           AFFIDAVIT OF SERVICE BY MAIL
COUNTY OF CLAY              )


    Student's name, being duly sworn, deposes and says that on
the second day of July, 19xx, she served the attached

            SUMMONS ◀── INSERT NAME OF DOCUMENT BEING SERVED


upon
                                         INSERT NAME OF
    ◀── THREE ──▶ Donald A. Mason ◀── PERSON BEING
       5-SPACE TABS                       SERVED

attorneys for plaintiff by placing a true and correct copy thereof in
an envelope addressed as follows:

INSERT
APPROPRIATE      Donald A. Mason
INFORMATION      MASON & FALLON          INSERT NAME
REGARDING        Attorneys at Law        AND ADDRESS OF
PERSON           1900 Smith Road         PERSON BEING
BEING            Moorhead, MN  56560-0099 SERVED
SERVED

and depositing the same, with postage prepaid, in the United States
mail at Moorhead, Minnesota.

         ↖
            INSERT APPROPRIATE
            MAILING SITE


                        _____
                        Secretary

    Subscribed and sworn to before me this _____ day of
_____, 19xx.




                        _____
    INSERT APPROPRIATE ──▶ Diana B. Perez, Notary Public
    NAME OF NOTARY,         Clay County, Minnesota
    COUNTY AND STATE,       My commission expires:  3-6-96
    AND COMMISSION
    EXPIRATION DATE
```

## Last Will and Testament

A last will and testament is a document that states the manner in which a person's property is to be distributed after death. Some of the clauses that may be included in a will are discussed in the following paragraphs.

**Introductory clause.** The introductory clause states the name of the testator or testatrix. It also states that the testator or testatrix is of sound mind, that he or she is acting of his or her own free will, and that the document is his or her last will and testament.

**Payment of debt clause.** The payment of debt clause directs the executor or executrix to pay all debts and funeral expenses as soon as possible.

**Distribution clause.** The distribution clause indicates the amount and type of property and to whom the property is left. There may be several distribution paragraphs, depending on the number of bequests.

**Trust clause.** The trust clause appoints a trustee to manage and distribute the funds or property left in trust for minor children or heirs of any age (heirs do not receive the total money or property at the time of the testator's or testatrix's death).

**Guardianship clause.** The guardianship clause appoints a person or institution to be responsible for the interests of minor children or incompetent adults in the estate.

**Testimonium clause.** The testimonium clause precedes the signature of the testator or testatrix. It takes the following form: IN WITNESS WHEREOF, I have hereunto set my hand and seal this 2nd day of August, 19xx.

**Attestation clause.** All states require that wills be executed in the presence of at least two witnesses. In addition to witnessing the execution of the will, the witnesses are asked to attest to the fact that the testator or testatrix is of sound mind at the time of signing. The signatures of all witnesses must appear on the same page as the signature of the testator or testatrix. If all these signature lines do not fit on one page, the first line of the testimonium clause goes on the last page of the will, the remainder of the page gets a *Z* ruling. The testimonium and attestation clauses are then concluded on the next page. Each page of a will should carry a page number ½ inch from the bottom of the page. The most often used style of page numbering is *Page 1 of 3.*

**Codicils to wills.** A testator or testatrix may change a portion of the will after it has been signed by executing a separate document called a *codicil.* The codicil makes reference to the date and number of pages of the original will, indicating the exact page number and paragraph that has been changed. The codicil is signed and witnessed in the same manner as the original will but does not necessarily require the same witnesses. No erasures in names and dollar amounts are permitted in the preparation of a will or codicil. A sample will is illustration in Figure 13.

**FIGURE 13**
Sample Last Will and Testament

LAST WILL AND TESTAMENT
OF
CAROLYN T. BLAKE


I, CAROLYN T. BLAKE, of the City of Moorhead, County of Clay, State of Minnesota, being of sound mind and disposing memory, do make, publish, and declare this to be my Last Will and Testament and hereby revoke any and all former Wills and Codicils heretofore made by me.

ARTICLE I.

I direct that all of my debts and my funeral expenses be paid as soon as practicable after my death.

ARTICLE II.

I give and devise my homestead and any other property that I may own at the time of my death to my husband, BRADY M. BLAKE.  Should my husband not survive me, any property that I may own at the time of my death shall be added to and distributed with the residue of my estate.

ARTICLE III.

All the rest, residue, and remainder of my property, real, personal, or mixed, wheresoever situated, I give and devise to my

Page 1 of 2

**FIGURE 13** (continued)

daughter, MARIA ELIZABETH ANDERSON, or to her issue by right of

representation.

_____

CAROLYN T. BLAKE

On this 2nd day of August, 19xx, CAROLYN T. BLAKE signed the
foregoing instrument and each page thereof in our presence and declared
it to be her Last Will and Testament, and as witnesses thereto, we do
now, at her request, in her presence, and in the presence of each
other, hereunto subscribe our names.

_____ residing at _____

_____ residing at _____

Page 2 of 2

**Land descriptions.** The guidelines that follow apply to the keyboarding of land descriptions. Refer to Figure 14 for a sample real estate document.

1. In towns and subdivisions, the *lot and block identification* is used.

   Example:   Lot Thirty-three (33), Block One (1), Mosset's Addition to the City of Moorhead, Clay County, Minnesota.

   Capitalize the words *lot* and *block*, the number of the lot and block, and the name of the subdivision or addition.

2. *U.S. Government Survey descriptions* are based on a rectangular survey system that first divides land into squares and squares within squares and then subdivides it into sections and townships. Survey descriptions are keyed as follows:

   Example:   The West Half of the Northwest Quarter (W1/2NW1/4) of Section Three (3), Township Forty-one (41) North, Range Thirty-nine (39) West of the Fifth Principal Meridian.

3. *Metes and bounds descriptions* measure land by courses and distances from a starting point. They are keyed as follows:

   Example:   Beginning at the Northeast Corner of the Southwest Quarter of the Southwest Quarter (SW1/4SW1/4) of Section Four (4) Township Thirteen (13) North, Range Four (4) West, James County, Minnesota, according to the United States Government Survey thereof; thence proceed East along the North Line of the SW1/4 of SW1/4 to an intersection with the West Line of the East Half of said SW1/4 of SW1/4; thence South along said West Line two hundred fifty-nine and fifty-five one hundredths (259.55) feet to a point and corner; thence South fifty-six degrees, nine minutes, thirty-three seconds West (South 56°09′33″ West) to an intersection with the West Line of said SW1/4 of SW1/4; thence North along the Quarter Line sixty-seven and seven tenths (67.7) feet to the point of beginning.

4. Capitalize specific directions such as north, northeast, south, west, southwest, etc., with initial capitals. Do not capitalize general directions such as northerly, northeasterly, etc.

5. Capitalize quarter, township, section, range, corner, line, and the name or number of a prime meridian.

   Example:   Fifth Principal Meridian

6. Key courses as follows:

   Example:   South forty degrees, twenty-three minutes, thirty-nine seconds West (South 40°23′39″ West)

   The single quotation mark stands for minutes; the double quotation mark stands for seconds.

7. Key distances as follows:

   Example:   two hundred twenty-nine and thirty-three one hundredths (229.33) feet

## FIGURE 14
Sample Real Estate Document Using a Preprinted Contract for Deed Form

1510—CONTRACT FOR DEED.  Individual to Individual.

THIS AGREEMENT, Made and entered into this........1st........day of.....April....., 19..XX.., by and between......Richard Grant........ part.y.... of the first part, and........Wayne J. Carlyle....................................................................................................part.y.... of the second part; whose post office address is........9168 Oak Street, Fargo................, State of North Dakota.......

WITNESSETH, That the said part.y.... of the first part, in consideration of the covenants and agreements of said part..y... of the second part, hereinafter contained, hereby sell.s.... and agree.s..... to convey unto said part.y.... of the second part or ....his..........................assigns, by a.................Warranty...................Deed, accompanied by an abstract evidencing good title in part.y.... of the first part at the date hereof, upon the prompt and full performance by said part..y.... of the second part, of ......... part of this agreement, the tract........ of land, lying and being in the County of .......Cass.....................and State of North Dakota, described as follows, to-wit:

```
Lot Sixteen (16), Block Eight (8),
Monterey First Addition to the
City of Fargo, County of Cass,
State of North Dakota
```

And said party.... of the second part, in consideration of the premises, hereby agree.s... to pay said part.y.. of the first part, at .....Fargo, North Dakota,...............as and for the purchase price of said premises, the sum of .......Twenty Thousand ($20,000)------------------------------------------Dollars, in manner and at times following, to-wit:

```
In consecutive monthly installments of Six Hundred
Twenty-six and 72/100 Dollars ($626.72) commencing
on the 1st day of May, 19xx, and a like sum on the
1st day of each month thereafter until the principal
and interest are fully paid, except that the final
payment of principal and interest, if not sooner
paid, shall be due and payable on January 1, 19xx.
The unpaid balance shall bear interest at the
initial rate of eight (8) percent per annum.
```

Said part..y.... of the second part further covenant.s.... and agree.s.... as follows: to pay, before penalty attaches thereto, all taxes due and payable in the year 19.XX., and in subsequent years, and all special assessments heretofore or hereafter levied upon said premises .....including sewer assessments in the sum of One Thousand Two Hundred Ninety-five Dollars ($1,295)-------------------------------- also that any buildings and improvements now on said land, or which shall hereafter be erected, placed, or made thereon, shall not be removed therefrom, but shall be and remain the property of the part.y..... of the first part until this contract shall be fully performed by the party.... of the second part; and at.his own expense, to keep the buildings on said premises at all times insured in some reliable insurance company or companies, to be approved by the part.y.... of the first part, against loss by fire, windstorm and hail...............................

for at least the sum of.......Twenty Thousand Dollars ($20,000)-----------------------Dollars, payable to said part.y.... of the first part, ....his...................heirs or assigns, and, in case of loss, should there be any surplus over and above the amount then owing said part..y.... of the first part, ..his..................heirs, or assigns, the balance shall be paid over to the said part.y.... of the second part as .his interest shall appear, and to deposit with the part.y.... of the first part policies of said insurance. But should the second part.y..... fail to pay any item to be paid by said part..y... under the terms hereof, same may be paid by first part.y.... and shall be forthwith payable, with interest thereon, as an additional amount due first part.y..... under this contract.

But should default be made in the payment of principal or interest due hereunder, or of any part thereof, to be by second part..y... paid, or should ..he. fail to pay the taxes or assessments upon said land, premiums

**FIGURE 14** (continued)

upon said insurance, or to perform any or either of the covenants, agreements, terms or conditions herein contained, to be by said second part..y... kept or performed, the said part..y.... of the first part may, at.....his........ option, by written notice declare this contract cancelled and terminated, and all rights, title and interest acquired thereunder by said second part.y....., shall thereupon cease and terminate, and all improvements made upon the premises, and all payments made hereunder shall belong to said part..y... of the first part as liquidated damages for breach of this contract by said second part..y...., said notice to be in accordance with the statute in such case made and provided. Neither the extension of the time of payment of any sum or sums of money to be paid hereunder, nor any waiver by the part.y..... of the first part of......his.................rights to declare this contract forfeited by reason of any breach thereof, shall in any manner affect the right of said part.y.... to cancel this contract because of defaults subsequently occurring, and no extension of time shall be valid unless evidenced by duly signed instrument. Further, after service of notice and failure to remove, within the period allowed by law, the default therein specified, said part.y..... of the second part hereby specifically agree, upon demand of said part..y.... of the first part, quietly and peaceably to surrender to........his.......................... possession of said premises, and every part thereof, it being understood that until such default, said part.y..... of the second part ........ to have possession of said premises.

IT IS MUTUALLY AGREED, By and between the parties hereto, that the time of payment shall be an essential part of this contract; and that all the covenants and agreements herein contained shall extend, run with the land, and bind the heirs, executors, administrators and assigns of the respective parties hereto.

IN TESTIMONY WHEREOF, The parties hereto have set their hands the day and year first above written.

In Presence of

Richard Grant

Wayne J. Carlyle

STATE OF NORTH DAKOTA, } ss.
County of.....Cass

On this.......1st.......day of.....April...................., 19XX....., before me
a.....Notary Public.......................................within and for said County, personally appeared
Richard Grant and Wayne J. Carlyle

to me known to be the person.s.. described in, and who executed the foregoing instrument, and acknowledged that .t..he.y... executed the same.

Susan A. Barnes
Notary Public...................Cass...........County, N. Dak.
My commission expires.......September 26..............., 19.XX...

**Contract for Deed**
Individual To Individual

Doc. No.

TO

Office of Register of Deeds

STATE OF NORTH DAKOTA,

County of.......

I hereby certify that the within Instrument was filed in this office for record on the........day of........19...., at........o'clock........M., and was duly recorded in Book........of........page........

Register of Deeds.

By........Deputy.

# UNDERSTANDING LATIN
# WORDS AND PHRASES

| WORDS | DEFINITIONS |
| --- | --- |
| a fortiori | From the most powerful reasoning; inference that if one conclusion or fact is true, then a second related fact or conclusion must be true |
| a priori | From cause to effect; deducing facts that must necessarily follow an admitted truth |
| ab initio | From the beginning; from the first act |
| ad curiam | At a court; to court |
| ad hoc | For this; for this special purpose |
| ad infinitum | Without limit; indefinitely; forever |
| ad litem | For the suit; for the litigation<br>*Guardian ad litem*: A person appointed by the Court to prosecute or to defend on behalf of a minor for the purpose of the lawsuit. |
| ad valorem | According to value |
| amicus curiae | Friend of the court |
| assumpsit | He undertook; he promised |
| bona fide | In or with good faith |
| caveat | Let him beware (a warning) |
| caveat emptor | Let the buyer beware |
| certiorari | To be informed of means of gaining appellate review<br>*Writ of certiorari*: If the writ is denied (cert. denied), the court refuses to hear the appeal, and in effect, the judgment below stands unchanged. If the writ is granted, then it has the effect of ordering the lower court to certify the record and send it up to the higher court to hear the appeal. |
| confer (cf.) | Compare |
| consortium | The conjugal fellowship of husband and wife and the right of each to the company, cooperation, and aid of the other in every conjugal relation |
| contra | Against |
| corpus | Body |
| corpus delicti | Body of the crime; objective proof that a crime has been committed |

| WORDS | DEFINITIONS |
|---|---|
| corpus juris | Body of the law |
| de facto | In fact; in reality; actually |
| de jure | By right: legitimate; lawful |
| de novo | Anew; afresh<br>*Trial de novo*: A new trial, as if no decision had previously been rendered. |
| duces tecum | Bring with you<br>*Subpoena duces tecum*: Order of the court requiring the witness to bring to court any relevant documents under witness's control. |
| erratum | Error |
| estoppel | A bar to denying a fact that has been settled by judicial proceeding or by one's own act or words |
| et alii<br>(et al.) | And others |
| et sequentes<br>(et seq.) | And the following |
| et uxor<br>(et ux.) | And wife |
| et vir | And husband |
| ex officio | From office; by virtue of the office |
| ex parte | On one side only; by or for one party<br>*Ex parte application*: Application to the court for the benefit of only one party without notice to or challenge by an adverse party. |
| flagrante delicto | In the very act of committing a crime |
| habeas corpus | You have the body<br>*Writ of habeas corpus*: A writ directed to the person detaining another, commanding that the body of the person detained be produced. |
| honorarium | Fee or gift; compensation from gratitude |
| ibidem<br>(ibid.) | In the same place; used in citations to mean "in the same book" or "on the same page" to avoid repeating source data immediately preceding |
| idem sonans<br>(id.) | Exactly the same; used in citations to avoid repeating author's name and title when reference to an item immediately follows another reference to same item |
| id est<br>(i.e.) | That is |
| in camera | In chambers; in private |
| indicia | Signs; indications |
| infra | Below; under; beneath |
| in limine | At the very beginning; preliminary<br>*Motion in limine*: Motion made before or after |

| WORDS | DEFINITIONS |
|---|---|
| | the beginning of a jury trial for a protective order against irrelevant, inadmissible, or prejudicial evidence. |
| in loco | In place |
| in personam | Proceedings against the person |
| in propria persona (in pro. per) | In one's own proper person (representing oneself) |
| in re | In the matter of; in regard |
| in rem | Proceedings against the thing |
| in toto | In the whole; completely |
| inter alia | Among other things |
| inter vivos | Between the living |
| intra | Within; during; between |
| ipso facto | By the fact itself |
| laches | Signifies an undue lapse of time in asserting right or claim |
| lis pendens | A pending suit<br>*Notice of lis pendens*: Notice on public record warning all persons that the title to certain property is in litigation and that any interest to the property is subject to the decision of the court. |
| locus delicti | Place where wrong occurred |
| mandamus | We command<br>*Writ of mandamus*: Order requiring performance of an official duty. |
| nolo contendere | I will not contest it |
| non compos mentis | Not of sound mind |
| non obstante verdico (n.o.v.) | Notwithstanding a verdict |
| non sequitur (non seq.) | It does not follow; logically incoherent |
| nota bene (N.B.) | Note well |
| nunc pro tunc | Now for then |
| pendente lite | Pending the suit; during litigation |
| per annum | By the year |
| per capita | By the head; as individuals |
| per curiam | By the court |
| per diem | By the day |
| per se | By itself; taken alone |
| post mortem | After death |
| prima facie | At first sight; on the face of it |

| WORDS | DEFINITIONS |
|---|---|
| pro forma | As a matter of form |
| pro hac vice | For this turn; for this one particular occasion |
| pro rata | According to the rate or proportion |
| pro tempore (pro tem.) | For the time being; temporarily |
| quasi | As if; as it were |
| quid pro quo | What for what; something for something |
| re | In the matter of; in the case of; regarding |
| res ipsa loquitur | The thing speaks for itself |
| res judicata | A matter judicated |
| scilicet (ss.) | To wit; that is to say |
| stare decises | To abide by decided cases (precedent; previously decided cases) |
| status quo | Existing state of things |
| supersedeas | You shall forbear<br>*Writ of supersedeas*: An official order halting or delaying proceedings of law. |
| supra | Above; refers reader to preceding part |
| versus (vs., v.) | Against |
| vis a vis | Face to face; in relation to each other |
| voir dire | To speak the truth; preliminary examination by attorneys to determine qualification of jury candidates |

Source: *Black's Law Dictionary*, 6th ed. (St. Paul, MN: West Publishing Company, 1990), 61–1575.

# CASE 1
# MECHANIC'S LIEN

| PLAINTIFF | DEFENDANT |
|---|---|
| David Navarro<br>85 24th Avenue North<br>Fargo, ND 58102-1234 | William T. Hillis<br>6051 Carpenter Avenue<br>Moorhead, MN 56560-2009 |
| **PLAINTIFF'S ATTORNEY** | **DEFENDANT'S ATTORNEY** |
| Barbara L. Walker<br>STEFANSEN, COHEN &<br>  SKRAMSTAD<br>3201 Interstate Avenue<br>Fargo, ND 58103-8773<br>(701) 555-1294<br>Minnesota License #968304<br>Office File Number: BLW67301-90 | Arthur C. Hastings<br>MAXWELL & HASTINGS<br>902 Center Avenue<br>Moorhead, MN 56560-1532<br>(218) 555-3924<br>Minnesota License #347296<br>Office File Number: ACH2950-91 |

**CASE SUMMARY**

In a mechanic's lien action, a worker (Navarro) files a claim against real property (machine repair shop) until the money owed for work done is paid. The plaintiff entered into a contract with the defendant to perform contracting services in the construction of a machine repair shop located in Clay County, Minnesota. The defendant has not paid the plaintiff for the services he performed; therefore, the plaintiff is attaching a mechanic's lien to the property (machine repair shop) to recover the money due and owing to him.

**SPECIAL INSTRUCTIONS**

1.  Use this caption on all court documents:

```
STATE OF MINNESOTA                        IN DISTRICT COURT

COUNTY OF CLAY                       SEVENTH JUDICIAL DISTRICT


David Navarro,
                                )
                 Plaintiff,     )    CIVIL NO. _____
                                )
        vs.                     )    NAME OF DOCUMENT
                                )
William T. Hillis and John      )
Does I and II, whose true       )
names are unknown to the        )
plaintiff,                      )
                                )
                 Defendants.    )
_____ )
```

2. Use this signature block on all legal documents:

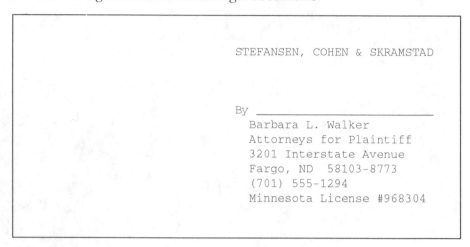

STEFANSEN, COHEN & SKRAMSTAD


By _____
Barbara L. Walker
Attorneys for Plaintiff
3201 Interstate Avenue
Fargo, ND 58103-8773
(701) 555-1294
Minnesota License #968304

**DOCUMENTS INCLUDED**

1. Summons
2. Complaint
3. Exhibit A
4. Letter to Barbara L. Walker
5. Letter to Defendant
6. Letter to Barbara L. Walker
7. Letter to Arthur C. Hastings
8. Letter to Barbara L. Walker
9. Letter to Barbara L. Walker
10. Letter to Arthur C. Hastings
11. Stipulation of Dismissal
12. Release Form
13. Letter to Defendant
14. Production Test for Case 1—Exhibit A

**MECHANIC'S LIEN FORECLOSURE TERMINOLOGY**

| WORDS | DEFINITIONS |
| --- | --- |
| adjudge | To decide or rule upon judicially |
| affiant | A person who executes an affidavit |
| bill of particulars | A detailed statement of charges or claims made by the plaintiff and given upon the defendant's request |
| counteroffer | An offer made by the offeree modifying or changing the offer made by the offeror; acts as an automatic rejection of original offer |
| duly | In a due manner, time, or degree; properly |
| equitable | Dealing fairly and equally with all concerned |
| foreclosure | An action to repossess real property |
| John Doe | A fictitious name used (1) in lawsuits where the name of a defendant is unknown or (2) to protect a person's identity |
| litigation | A lawsuit or series of lawsuits |
| mechanic's lien | A worker's or contractor's claim against real |

| WORDS | DEFINITIONS |
|---|---|
| | property for money owed on work performed in or on said real property |
| offer | To make a proposal |
| per annum | By the year; each year |
| premises | A tract of land with the buildings thereon |
| release form | A paper giving up or relinquishing a claim or a right by the person who signs it |
| relief | The help given by a court to a person who brings a lawsuit (the relief asked for might be the return of property, enforcement of a contract, or payment of money) |
| settlement | An agreement about a debt, payment of a debt, or disposition of a lawsuit |
| statute | A law passed by a legislature |
| stipulation of dismissal with prejudice | Agreement to dismiss an action and bar any future lawsuit on same the cause of action |
| stipulation of dismissal without prejudice | Agreement to dismiss an action without affecting the right to bring a later lawsuit on the same cause of action |
| subordinate | To treat as of less value or importance |
| tender | To present for acceptance |
| third party | A person who may be brought into an existing law-suit by the defendant |

Source: Daniel Oran, J.D., *Law Dictionary for Nonlawyers*, 2nd ed. (St. Paul, MN: West Publishing Company, 1985).

stefansen
cohen &
skramstad

**Attorneys at Law**

Gail S. Stefansen, Bernard J. Cohen, Ann D. Skramstad
HOME OFFICE: 3201 Interstate Avenue, Fargo, ND  58103-8773 (701) 555-1294

Neil W. Webster, Barbara L. Walker, Tomas J. Lopez
SATELLITE OFFICE: 2213 Roosevelt Avenue, Moorhead, MN  56560-9909 (218) 555-1781

stefansen
cohen &
skramstad

**Attorneys at Law**

Gail S. Stefansen, Bernard J. Cohen, Ann D. Skramstad
HOME OFFICE: 3201 Interstate Avenue, Fargo, ND  58103-8773 (701) 555-1294

Neil W. Webster, Barbara L. Walker, Tomas J. Lopez
SATELLITE OFFICE: 2213 Roosevelt Avenue, Moorhead, MN  56560-9909 (218) 555-1781

39

# M&H

## MAXWELL & HASTINGS
*902 Center Avenue • Moorhead, MN • 56560-1532 • (218) 555-3924*

# M&H

## MAXWELL & HASTINGS
902 Center Avenue • Moorhead, MN • 56560-1532 • (218) 555-3924

# M&H

**MAXWELL & HASTINGS**
902 Center Avenue • Moorhead, MN • 56560-1532 • (218) 555-3924

# M&H

MAXWELL & HASTINGS
902 Center Avenue • Moorhead, MN • 56560-1532 • (218) 555-3924

# CASE 2
# CREDIT, COLLECTION, AND DEFAULT JUDGMENT

## PLAINTIFF

Joshua Hamilton, dba
Hamilton Trailer Sales
1324 Main Avenue
Fargo, ND 58102-0404

## PLAINTIFF'S ATTORNEY

Barbara L. Walker
STEFANSEN, COHEN &
  SKRAMSTAD
3201 Interstate Avenue
Fargo, ND 58103-8773
(701) 555-1294
North Dakota License #213784
Office File Number: BLW2146-90

## DEFENDANT

Jason P. Edwards
Jill R. Edwards
4121 Bluemont Court
Casselton, ND 58012-2273

## DEFENDANTS' ATTORNEY

The defendants, who have not
retained an attorney, have made no
responsive answer, which will place
the case into default.

**CASE SUMMARY**

Joshua Hamilton, the plaintiff in this case, sold a mobile home to the defendants (Account #21425). After two years of trying to collect payment on the mobile home, Mr. Hamilton repossessed it and engaged a lawyer to collect the balance due. A lawsuit was initiated. Mr. and Mrs. Edwards still refused to pay and they have not sought legal counsel to represent them. This inaction allowed the case to go into default after the elapse of a 20-day period following the service of the summons and complaint. After receiving judgment on the complaint, garnishment proceedings were begun. The Sheriff again served a summons and a garnishment affidavit on Mr. and Mrs. Edwards and on D & H Construction Company of West Fargo, North Dakota, the employer of both Mr. and Mrs. Edwards. After being served with the garnishment papers, the defendants paid the indebtedness in full. A garnishment release was then prepared and delivered by the Sheriff, releasing the defendants and D & H Construction Company from further action.

1. Use this caption on all documents pertaining to the initial litigation of this case (i.e., for the collection portion):

```
        IN DISTRICT COURT, CASS COUNTY, NORTH DAKOTA


Joshua Hamilton, dba          )
Hamilton Trailer Sales,       )
                              )
              Plaintiff,      )    CIVIL NO. _____
                              )
        vs.                   )    NAME OF DOCUMENT
                              )
Jason P. Edwards and          )
Jill R. Edwards, his wife,    )
                              )
              Defendants.     )
_____)
```

2. Use this caption for the documents pertaining to the garnishment proceedings:

```
        IN DISTRICT COURT, CASS COUNTY, NORTH DAKOTA


Joshua Hamilton, dba          )
Hamilton Trailer Sales,       )
                              )
              Plaintiff,      )    CIVIL NO. _____
                              )
        vs.                   )    GARNISHEE SUMMONS AND
                              )    NOTICE to DEFENDANT
Jason P. Edwards and          )
Jill R. Edwards, his wife,    )    (Continuing Lien)
                              )
        Judgment Debtors,     )
                              )
        and                   )
                              )
D & H Construction Company,   )
                              )
              Garnishee.      )
_____)
```

3.  Use this signature block on all legal documents prepared by Ms. Walker:

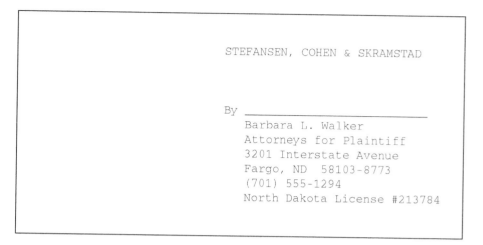

```
                            STEFANSEN, COHEN & SKRAMSTAD



                     By _____
                            Barbara L. Walker
                            Attorneys for Plaintiff
                            3201 Interstate Avenue
                            Fargo, ND  58103-8773
                            (701) 555-1294
                            North Dakota License #213784
```

**DOCUMENTS INCLUDED**

1. Letter to Defendants
2. Letter to Defendants
3. Verification of Debt and Statement and Affidavit of Service by Mail
4. Letter to Sheriff
5. Summons and Complaint
6. Letter to Clerk of District Court
7. Affidavit of No Answer
8. Affidavit of Identification and Non-Military Service
9. Affidavit of Proof
10. Order for Default Judgment on Failure to Answer
11. Judgment on Failure to Answer
12. Statement of Judgment Disbursements and Costs
13. Letter to Clerk of District Court
14. Notice of Entry of Judgment and Affidavit of Service by Mail
15. Notice of Garnishment of Earnings and Affidavit of Service by Mail
16. Letter to Sheriff
17. Garnishee Summons and Notice to Defendants
18. Letter to Plaintiff
19. Satisfaction of Judgment
20. Production Test for Case 2—Summons

**CREDIT, COLLECTION, AND DEFAULT JUDGMENT TERMINOLOGY**

| WORDS | DEFINITIONS |
|---|---|
| adduce | Present evidence in a trial |
| adjudge | To rule or decide upon judicially |
| affiant | A person who executes an affidavit |
| affidavit | A written, signed statement of facts sworn to before a notary public |
| allege | To state, assert, or charge |
| annex | To attach, append, or add a statement or document to another document |
| creditor | A person to whom money is owed |

| WORDS | DEFINITIONS |
|---|---|
| dba or d/b/a | Abbreviation used for doing business as |
| debtor | A person who owes money |
| decree | A judgment of the Court that announces the legal consequences of the facts found in a case and orders that the Court's decision be carried out |
| default | A failure to perform a legal duty, observe a promise, fulfill an obligation, or pay a debt when due |
| demurrer | To stop or stay an action; a formal objection attacking the legal sufficiency of a pleading (in many jurisdictions, the demurrer has been replaced by a motion to dismiss) |
| execution | The process of carrying out a Court's order or judgment (e.g., collection of the money ordered paid) |
| express | Clear, definite, direct, or actual; explicit words |
| garnishee | The person who holds money or property belonging to a debtor and who is subject to proceedings by a creditor |
| garnishment | A legal proceeding taken by a creditor after judgment to compel the garnishee to turn over money or property belonging to a debtor |
| implied | Known indirectly |
| judgment by default | A court order granting judgment to the defendant because the defendant fails to appear in action or answer the complaint |
| jurisdiction | The limits and territory within which the court's authority may be exercised |
| legal rate of interest | Rate of interest set by the state that may be charged on money owed when the interest rate is not stated in the contract |
| Notary Public | A public official who can administer oaths, certify the validity of documents, and perform other types of witnessing duties |
| per annum | By the year; each year |
| personal property | Movable property |
| premise | A proposition upon which an argument is based or from which a conclusion is drawn |
| pursuant | In accordance with; in carrying out |
| real property | Land and things attached to land, such as buildings |
| return of service | Statement by the Sheriff giving the name of the person served, the date, the place, and the manner of service of a document or an explanation of why service could not be completed (similar to an affidavit of service) |

| WORDS | DEFINITIONS |
|---|---|
| Sheriff | Chief law officer of a county in charge of serving process, calling jurors, keeping the peace, executing judgments, etc. |
| statute | A law passed by a legislature |
| venue | The local area where a case may be tried |

Source: Daniel Oran, J.D., *Law Dictionary for Nonlawyers*, 2nd ed. (St. Paul, MN: West Publishing Company, 1985).

stefansen
cohen &
skramstad

**Attorneys at Law**

Gail S. Stefansen, Bernard J. Cohen, Ann D. Skramstad
HOME OFFICE: 3201 Interstate Avenue, Fargo, ND  58103-8773 (701) 555-1294

Neil W. Webster, Barbara L. Walker, Tomas J. Lopez
SATELLITE OFFICE: 2213 Roosevelt Avenue, Moorhead, MN  56560-9909 (218) 555-1781

stefansen
cohen &
skramstad

**Attorneys at Law**

Gail S. Stefansen, Bernard J. Cohen, Ann D. Skramstad
HOME OFFICE: 3201 Interstate Avenue, Fargo, ND  58103-8773 (701) 555-1294

Neil W. Webster, Barbara L. Walker, Tomas J. Lopez
SATELLITE OFFICE: 2213 Roosevelt Avenue, Moorhead, MN  56560-9909 (218) 555-1781

Case 2

61

stefansen
cohen &
skramstad

**Attorneys at Law**

Gail S. Stefansen, Bernard J. Cohen, Ann D. Skramstad
HOME OFFICE: 3201 Interstate Avenue, Fargo, ND 58103-8773 (701) 555-1294

Neil W. Webster, Barbara L. Walker, Tomas J. Lopez
SATELLITE OFFICE: 2213 Roosevelt Avenue, Moorhead, MN 56560-9909 (218) 555-1781

stefansen
cohen &
skramstad

**Attorneys at Law**

Gail S. Stefansen, Bernard J. Cohen, Ann D. Skramstad
HOME OFFICE: 3201 Interstate Avenue, Fargo, ND  58103-8773 (701) 555-1294

Neil W. Webster, Barbara L. Walker, Tomas J. Lopez
SATELLITE OFFICE: 2213 Roosevelt Avenue, Moorhead, MN  56560-9909 (218) 555-1781

Case 2

65

stefansen
cohen &
skramstad

**Attorneys at Law**

Gail S. Stefansen, Bernard J. Cohen, Ann D. Skramstad
HOME OFFICE: 3201 Interstate Avenue, Fargo, ND 58103-8773 (701) 555-1294

Neil W. Webster, Barbara L. Walker, Tomas J. Lopez
SATELLITE OFFICE: 2213 Roosevelt Avenue, Moorhead, MN 56560-9909 (218) 555-1781

stefansen
cohen &
skramstad

**Attorneys at Law**

Gail S. Stefansen, Bernard J. Cohen, Ann D. Skramstad
HOME OFFICE: 3201 Interstate Avenue, Fargo, ND 58103-8773 (701) 555-1294

Neil W. Webster, Barbara L. Walker, Tomas J. Lopez
SATELLITE OFFICE: 2213 Roosevelt Avenue, Moorhead, MN 56560-9909 (218) 555-1781

stefansen
cohen &
skramstad

**Attorneys at Law**

Gail S. Stefansen, Bernard J. Cohen, Ann D. Skramstad
HOME OFFICE: 3201 Interstate Avenue, Fargo, ND  58103-8773 (701) 555-1294

Neil W. Webster, Barbara L. Walker, Tomas J. Lopez
SATELLITE OFFICE: 2213 Roosevelt Avenue, Moorhead, MN  56560-9909 (218) 555-1781

# CASE 3
# LEGAL POTPOURRI

**ATTORNEY FOR CASE**

Tomas J. Lopez
STEFANSEN, COHEN & SKRAMSTAD
3201 Interstate Avenue
Fargo, ND  58103-8773
(701) 555-1294
North Dakota License #345876

**CASE SUMMARY**

The term *potpourri* means miscellaneous collection. This case represents a miscellaneous collection of legal proceedings. Tomas J. Lopez, of the law firm of STEFANSEN, COHEN & SKRAMSTAD, handles most of the miscellaneous legal work in the office. He is the attorney responsible for all items included in this case.

**SPECIAL INSTRUCTIONS**

1. Refer to the reference section if you have any questions about formatting the documents in this case.
2. For the employment agreement with nondisclosure provisions, the parties are Kevin P. Henderson of Medical Suppliers, Inc., employer, and Juli K. Morgan, employee.
3. The standard employment agreement is between Designs by Richard, the company, and Wayne J. Carlyle, the consultant.
4. The parties to the earnest money contract are Allen D. Emerson, seller and party of the first part, and Nicole D. Chamberlain, buyer and party of the second part.
5. The parties to the warranty deed are Allen D. Emerson, grantor, and Nicole D. Chamberlain, grantee.
6. The mortgage deed is between Kjersten C. Andrews, party of the first part, and Northwestern Bank and Trust Company, party of the second part.

**DOCUMENTS INCLUDED**

1. Employment Agreement with Extensive Nondisclosure Provisions
2. Employment Agreement
3. Earnest Money Contract (Preprinted Form Available)
4. Warranty Deed (Preprinted Form Available)
5. Mortgage Deed (Preprinted Form Available)
6. Production Test for Case 3—Satisfaction of Mortgage (Preprinted Form Available)

**LEGAL POTPOURRI TERMINOLOGY**

| WORDS | DEFINITIONS |
| --- | --- |
| appurtenance | Something that belongs to or is attached to something else (e.g., a barn on a farm) |
| assignee | Person to whom something is given or transferred |
| assignor | Person who gives or transfers something |

| WORDS | DEFINITIONS |
|---|---|
| bond | An obligation made binding by a money forfeiture |
| breach | Break a law or fail to perform a duty (e.g., a breach of contract is failure to perform any promise or to carry out any of the terms of a contract) |
| compensation | Payment for services rendered |
| confidentiality | A requirement that certain persons not disclose information received under certain circumstances (e.g., between lawyer and client) |
| construe | To understand or explain the sense or intention of |
| covenant | A written promise, agreement, or restriction |
| conveyance | A transfer of title to real property (land) |
| disclosure | The act of exposing or making information known to the public |
| easement | The right created by agreement of a specific non-owner to use the land of another in a particular way (e.g., the right of a telephone company to erect telephone poles and cables on your property and to enter your property to maintain the equipment) |
| encumbrance | A claim, charge, or liability on property such as a lien or mortgage |
| enjoin | Require, command, or forbid |
| entity | An independent, separate, or self-contained existence |
| grantee | The person to whom title to property is conveyed (party of the second part) |
| grantor | The person who conveys title to property (party of the first part) |
| injunction | A court order to a person to do or refrain from doing a particular thing |
| mortgage deed | A deed pledging real property as security for a loan made by a lending institution to the owner of the property |
| mortgagee | A person or lending institution to whom property is mortgaged (party of the second part) |
| mortgagor | The owner of the property (party of the first part) |
| restraining order | A judge's order prohibiting a person from taking certain action before a full hearing can be held on the question |
| right-of-way | Easement; a legal right of passage over another person's land (e.g., use of a private sidewalk, road, or path by the public) |
| supersede | Set aside; annul; make void; replace one law or document by another |
| therefor | For or in return for that (e.g., "I have received your invoice for $500 and the check therefor will be mailed immediately") |

| WORDS | DEFINITIONS |
|---|---|
| therefore | For that reason; consequently; because of that; on that ground; to that end |
| waiver | The voluntary giving up of a right |
| warranty deed | The document that guarantees that the title to the land being conveyed is free and clear of all claims, encumbrances, and liens |

Source: Daniel Oran, J.D., *Law Dictionary for Nonlawyers*, 2nd ed. (St. Paul, MN: West Publishing Company, 1985).

# EARNEST MONEY CONTRACT

THIS AGREEMENT, Made and entered into this_____day of_____, 19_____, by and between

_____

_____

whose post office address is_____,

part_____ of the first part, hereinafter called "Seller" and_____

whose post office address is_____, part_____ of the second part, hereinafter called "Buyer",

    WITNESSETH, That the seller agrees to sell and the buyer agrees to purchase, upon the terms and conditions hereinafter set forth, the following described real property and all appurtenances thereunto belonging, owned by the seller and located in

the County of_____, State of North Dakota, to-wit:

_____

_____

_____

_____

_____

Included in the sale of the above property is the following personal property:

_____

_____

    The terms and conditions of such sale and purchase are as follows:

The purchase price shall be_____

Dollars ($          ) payable as follows:_____

_____

_____

_____

_____

    The buyer has paid the sum of _____Dollars ($     ) as earnest money to be credited on purchase price, the receipt whereof is hereby acknowledged by the seller and agrees to perform the other

terms and conditions of this contract to be kept and performed by the buyer upon the delivery of a _____
deed by the seller, conveying said premises to the buyer or to such other persons as the buyer may designate.

    The seller shall furnish the buyer a duly certified abstract of title to said premises, continued to a recent date, showing good

and marketable title in the seller free and clear of all liens and encumbrances, except_____

_____

The seller agrees to pay all taxes and special assessments or assessments for special improvements due, levied or assessed for

the year _____ and prior years. Taxes, special assessments or assessments for special improvements for the year 19 _____,
shall be prorated between the buyer and the seller on the basis of the taxes, special assessments or assessments for special

improvements for the year 19_____. Buyer agrees to pay the taxes and special assessments or assessments for special improve-

ments for the year 19_____ and subsequent years._____

    The buyer shall have _____ days time to examine said abstract of title and within said period of time shall promptly notify the seller of all objections thereto in writing. If the title to such premises is unmarketable, the seller shall have a period

of _____ days in which to correct the title and make it marketable. If the title to said premises cannot be made marketable within said period of time or such further time as may be granted by the buyer, the buyer shall be entitled to the return of the earnest money paid under this contract, but otherwise this contract shall be wholly null, void and unenforcable. Should the buyer default in completing the terms and conditions of this earnest money contract, the earnest money paid by the buyer shall, at the option of the seller, be forfeited as liquidated damages.

    Possession of said premises shall be delivered to the buyer on the _____ day of_____

19_____, subject to the extension of time heretofore granted, in the event that title to such premises should be found unmarketable.

    This contract and the earnest money paid hereunder shall be held by_____
for the mutual benefit of the parties hereto.

    Time is of the essence of each provision of this entire contract and of all the conditions thereof.

    IN TESTIMONY WHEREOF, Said parties have hereunto set their hands the day and year first above written.

WITNESSES:                               SELLER:

_____      _____

_____      _____

                                         BUYER:

                                         _____

STATE OF

COUNTY OF  } ss.

On this_____day of_____, 19___, before me, a Notary Public, within and for said county and state, personally appeared_____known to me to be the person— who_____described in and who executed the within and foregoing instrument, and severally acknowledged that ___he__ executed the same.

_____
Notary Public.

(SEAL)  My commission expires:_____

STATE OF

COUNTY OF  } ss.

On this_____day of_____, 19___, before me, a Notary Public, within and for said county and state, personally appeared_____known to me to be the person___ who_____described in and who executed the within and foregoing instrument, and severally acknowledged that ___he__ executed the same.

_____
Notary Public.

(SEAL)  My commission expires:_____

STATE OF NORTH DAKOTA,

County of_____  } ss.

On this_____day of_____in the year 19_____, before me a Notary Public within and for said County and State, personally appeared before me,_____ _____and_____ known to me to be the_____President and_____Secretary of the corporation that is described in and that executed the within instrument and acknowledged to me that said corporation executed the same.

My commission expires:_____19_____  _____

Notary Public_____County,
N. Dak.

THIS INDENTURE, Made this.............................day of............................................., 19........, between

..............................................................................................................................................................................

...................................................................................................................................................grantor,

whether one or more, and............................................................................................................................

...................................................................................................................................................grantee.

whether one or more, whose post office address is............................................................................................

WITNESSETH, For and in consideration of the sum of.....................................................................

.................................................................................................................................................Dollars,

grantor does hereby GRANT to the grantee all of the following real property lying and being in the

County of.........................................., State of North Dakota, and described as follows, to-wit:

And the grantor for himself, his heirs, executors and administrators, does covenant with the grantee that he is well seized in fee of the land and premises aforesaid and has good right to sell and convey the same in manner and form aforesaid; that the same are free from all incumbrances, except installments of special assessments or assessments for special improvements which have not been certified to the

County Treasurer for collection,...........................................................................................................

..............................................................................................................................................................

and the above granted lands and premises in the quiet and peaceable possession of the grantee, against all persons lawfully claiming or to claim the whole or any part thereof, the grantor will warrant and defend.

WITNESS, The hand of the grantor:

In the presence of

..............................................................................          ..............................................................................

                                                                              ..............................................................................

..............................................................................          ..............................................................................

                                                                              ..............................................................................

STATE OF NORTH DAKOTA

COUNTY OF........................................................}  ss.

On this.......................day of............................................., 19........., before me personally appeared

..............................................................................................................................................................

.......................................................................................................................known to me to be

the person...... who ............. described in, and who executed the within and foregoing instrument, and

severally acknowledged that ................. executed the same.

My Commission Expires:

.......................................................................................          Notary Public,

................................................................., 19........

                                                                              .............................................County, N. Dak.

STATE OF NORTH DAKOTA

COUNTY OF........................................................}  ss.

I hereby certify that the within Deed was filed

in this office for record on the.....................................          Delinquent taxes and special assessments or

day of............................................., 19........,          installments of special assessments paid and

at...........................o'clock..........M., and was duly          transfer entered this..................................... day of

recorded as Document No. .....................................in          ................................................., 19........

Book......................of Deeds, Page...................

..............................................................................          ..............................................................................

                    Register of Deeds                                               County Auditor

By ...............................................................Deputy          By .................................................................Deputy

1532—MORTGAGE DEED—N.D. Standard Form. Mortgagee a Corporation. (Sec. 35-63-05. N.D.C.C. 1960)

**THIS INDENTURE,** Made this.................................day of..............................................

A. D., One thousand nine hundred...................................................................................between

...................................................................................................................................................

...................................................................................................................................................

whose postoffice address is.............................................................................................................

of the County of.........................................and State of North Dakota, part......... of the first part, and

...................................................................................................................................................

...........................................................................................................................a corporation

whose postoffice address is.............................................................................................................

of the County of.........................................and State of North Dakota, part......... of the second

WITNESSETH, That the said part.......... of the first part, for and in consideration of the sum of

.................................................................................................................................Dollars

to...............................................in hand paid by the said party of the second part, the receipt whereof is hereby

acknowledged, do........... by these presents Grant, Bargain, Sell and Convey to the said part........... of the.....
second part, its successors and assigns, forever, all the following described real estate in the County of

...................................................................and State of North Dakota, described as follows, to-wit:

...................................................................................................................................................

...................................................................................................................................................

...................................................................................................................................................

...................................................................................................................................................

...................................................................................................................................................

...................................................................................................................................................

TO HAVE AND TO HOLD THE SAME, Together with all the hereditaments and appurtenances thereunto belonging, or in anywise appertaining, unto the said party of the second part, its successors and

assigns, FOREVER. And the said part.................. of the first part, do........... covenant with the said part...........

of the second part, its successors and assigns, as follows: That ........he....... ha....... good right to convey the

same; that the same are free from all incumbrances.........................................................................

...................................................................................................................................................

...................................................................................................................................................

...................................................................................................................................................

.........................................................................and that the said part......... of the second part, its successors and
assigns shall quietly enjoy and possess the same, and that the said part.......... of the first part will warrant and
defend the title to the same against all lawful claims, hereby relinquishing and conveying all right of homestead,
dower and all contingent claims and rights whatsoever in and to the said premises.

**Mortgagee** reserves the right and upon request of the Mortgagor, Mortgagee, at Mortgagee's option,
shall have the right to advance funds or make additional loans to the Mortgagor as provided by Section
6-03-05.1 of the North Dakota Century Code.

PROVIDED, NEVERTHELESS, That if the said part.......... of the first part.......................heirs,

executors, administrators, successors or assigns, shall well and truly pay, or cause to be paid, to the said part.........

of the second part, its successors or assigns, the sum of.............................................................

.................................................................................................................Dollars and

interest according to the conditions of.........................................note......... of even date herewith, as follows,

...................................................................................................................................................

payable at the...............................................................................................................................
with interest from date until paid at the rate of.................per cent, per annum, interest payable annually, and shall
repay any future advance or loans as authorized herein, and shall also keep and perform all and singular the
covenants and agreements herein contained, then this deed to be null and void, and the premises hereby conveyed

to be released at the cost of the said part........ of the first part; otherwise to remain in full force and effect.

And the said part........... of the first part do........ covenant and agree with the said part........... of the second
part, its successors and assigns to pay the said sum of money and interest thereon as above specified; to pay
as a part of the debt hereby secured, in case of each or any foreclosure or commencement of foreclosure of this
mortgage, all costs and expenses and statutory attorney's fees in addition to all sums and costs allowed in that
behalf by law; to permit no waste, and to do or permit to be done, to said premises, nothing that may in any
manner impair or weaken the security under this mortgage; to pay all taxes or assessments that may be assessed

against or be a lien on said premises, or any part thereof, or upon this mortgage or note........ of the legal holder thereof, before the same shall become delinquent; to keep the buildings on said premises insured against loss by fire and windstorm and............................................................for at least....................................................

...............................................................................................................................................................................Dollars,

in companies acceptable to and with loss payable to, the mortgagee or.................................assigns; and in case of failure so to pay said taxes or assessments, or to comply with any of the agreements herein, or in case there exists

any claim, lien or incumbrance upon said premises, which is prior to this mortgage, the said part........... of the

second part, its successors or assigns may at.............................option, pay and discharge such taxes or other obligation and the sum or sums of money which may be so paid, with interest from time of payment at the same rate as said principal sum, shall be deemed and are hereby declared to be a part of the debt secured by this mortgage and shall be immediately due and payable. It is further agreed and understood that this mortgage shall also cover any renewal note for the above described indebtedness or any portion thereof.

But if default shall be made in the payment of said sum of money, or interest, or the taxes, or any part thereof, at the time and in the manner hereinbefore or hereinafter specified for the payment thereof, the said

part........... of the first part, in such cases do........... hereby authorize and fully empower the said part........... of the second part, its successors or assigns, to sell the said hereby granted premises and convey the same to the purchaser, in fee simple, agreeably to the statute in such case made and provided, and out of the moneys arising

from such sale to retain the principal and interest which shall then be due on said note........, and all taxes upon said lands, together with all costs and charges and statutory attorney's fees, and pay the overplus if any to the

said part........ of the first part, ........................ heirs, executors, administrators or assigns. And if default

be made by the part........... of the first part in any of the foregoing provisions it shall be lawful for the part...........

of the second part, its successors or assigns, or.................................................attorney to declare the whole sum above specified to be due.

IN TESTIMONY WHEREOF, the said part........... of the first part ha........ hereunto set ..........................

hand...... the day and year first above written.

Signed and Delivered in the Presence of

.........................................................

.........................................................

.........................................................

STATE OF NORTH DAKOTA,

County of...........................................}ss.

On this.............................day of.................................................in the year 19........., before me

personally appeared...........................................................................................................................

known to me to be the person...... who.................................................described in and who executed the within

instrument, and acknowledged to me that ........he.................................executed the same.

.........................................................

My commission expires.............................19.........        .........................................................

**THIS CERTIFIES,** That a certain Mortgage, executed by _____

of _____ , in the County of _____ , and State of North Dakota, to

_____

in the County of _____ and State of _____ , dated the

_____ day of _____ 19, _____, upon the _____

_____

_____

_____

and recorded in the office of the Register of Deeds in and for the County of _____ and

State of North Dakota, on the _____ day of _____ 19 _____, at _____ M, in Book _____ of

Mortgage Deeds, on page _____ or Document No. _____ , is paid and satisfied, with the notes accompanying

the same, and _____ hereby authorize and require said Register of Deeds for said County to

discharge the same of record in his office.

Witness _____ hand _____ this _____ day of _____ A.D., 19 _____ .

Signed, Sealed and Delivered in Presence of

_____          _____

_____          _____

STATE OF NORTH DAKOTA,  } ss.

County of _____

On this _____ day of _____ A.D., 19 _____, before me personally appeared

_____

known to me to be the same person____ described in and who executed the above and foregoing instrument,

and severally acknowledged that _____ he _____ executed the same.

_____

Notary Public in and for

My commission expires _____ 19, ____     _____ County, State of _____

# Satisfaction of Mortgage

TO

OFFICE OF REGISTER OF DEEDS

STATE OF NORTH DAKOTA,

County of ———— } ss.

I hereby certify that the within Satis-

faction of Mortgage was filed in this office

for record on the ———— day

of ———— A.D., 19 ——

at ———— o'clock ———— M., and was ————

duly recorded in Book ———— of ————

———— on page ————

By ————

Register of Deeds.

———— Deputy.

# CASE 4
# CHANGE OF VENUE

| PLAINTIFFS | DEFENDANT |
|---|---|
| Tony G. Wilson and<br>Georgia T. Kingston<br>5550 South Elm<br>Fargo, ND 58102-2990 | Conway Builders, Inc.<br>3490 Rensvold Road<br>Moorhead, MN 56560-8005 |
| **PLAINTIFFS' ATTORNEY** | **DEFENDANT'S ATTORNEY** |
| Gail S. Stefansen<br>STEFANSEN, COHEN &<br>   SKRAMSTAD<br>3201 Interstate Avenue<br>Fargo, ND 58103-8773<br>(701) 555-1294<br>North Dakota License #114601<br>Office File Number: GS861988 | Gregory North<br>NORTH, COX & HARMON<br>201 Dakota Building<br>Fargo, ND 58102-9638<br>(701) 555-7729<br>North Dakota License #503856<br>Office File Number: 6040597 |

**CASE SUMMARY**

This case involves an action for the removal of a lawsuit from state to federal court. The case was first venued in the District Court, State of North Dakota, County of Cass, but because of the amount of money involved, it is being removed to the United States District Court for the District of North Dakota.

The plaintiffs are in a partnership for the purpose of building an office complex located at 2204 Roosevelt Drive South, Fargo, North Dakota. They initiated a lawsuit against Conway Builders, Inc. for relief from damages incurred as a result of stress cracks in the improperly constructed brick structure, foundation, and footings.

You are working as the secretary to Gail S. Stefansen, of STEFANSEN, COHEN & SKRAMSTAD, the attorney for the plaintiffs. The opposing counsel, Gregory North, of NORTH, COX & HARMON, is attorney for the defendant.

1. Use this caption for documents in this action:

```
                    UNITED STATES DISTRICT COURT
                       DISTRICT OF NORTH DAKOTA
                           NINTH DIVISION


    Tony G. Wilson and               )
    Georgia T. Kingston,             )
                                     )
                     Plaintiffs,     )    CIVIL NO. _____
                                     )
         vs.                         )    NAME OF DOCUMENT
                                     )
    Conway Builders, Inc.,           )
                                     )
                     Defendant.      )
    _____    )
```

2. Use this signature block on all legal documents in this action:

```
                    STEFANSEN, COHEN & SKRAMSTAD



             By _____
                Gail S. Stefansen
                Attorneys for Plaintiffs
                3201 Interstate Avenue
                Fargo, ND  58103-8773
                (701) 555-1294
                North Dakota License #114601
```

**DOCUMENTS
INCLUDED**

1. Notice of Filing of Notice of Removal
2. Notice of Removal
3. Joinder in Notice of Removal with Affidavit of Service by Mail
4. Letter to Clerk of United States District Court
5. Clerk's Certificate of Filing
6. Letter to Clerk of the District Court
7. Letter to Opposing Counsel
8. Letter to Clerk of United States District Court
9. Production Test for Case 4—Memo

**CHANGE OF VENUE TERMINOLOGY**

| WORDS | DEFINITIONS |
|---|---|
| allegation | A statement in a pleading that one side expects to prove |
| controversy | Dispute, argument, or disagreement between parties |
| counsel | Lawyer; attorney |
| effect | To bring about; to cause to come into being |
| execute | Complete; make; perform; carry out |
| Federal District Court | Part of the federal court system in which matters involving federal laws are tried (the federal court having original, general jurisdiction, meaning that a civil or criminal action may be started in this court) |
| incorporate | To incorporate by reference is to make a part of something by mere reference |
| joinder | Joining or uniting |
| jurisdiction | The limits and territory within which the court's authority may be exercised |
| pleadings | The formal written documents or written statements by each side to a lawsuit; legal papers or documents |
| process | Any means used by the court to acquire jurisdiction over a person or property |
| pursuant | In accordance with; in carrying out |
| removal | The transfer of a case from state to federal court |
| statutory | Having to do with a statute; created, defined, or required by a statute |
| venue | The local area where a case may be tried |

Source: Daniel Oran, J.D., *Law Dictionary for Nonlawyers*, 2nd ed. (St. Paul, MN: West Publishing Company, 1985).

stefansen
cohen &
skramstad

**Attorneys at Law**

Gail S. Stefansen, Bernard J. Cohen, Ann D. Skramstad
HOME OFFICE: 3201 Interstate Avenue, Fargo, ND  58103-8773 (701) 555-1294

Neil W. Webster, Barbara L. Walker, Tomas J. Lopez
SATELLITE OFFICE: 2213 Roosevelt Avenue, Moorhead, MN  56560-9909 (218) 555-1781

stefansen
cohen &
skramstad

**Attorneys at Law**

Gail S. Stefansen, Bernard J. Cohen, Ann D. Skramstad
HOME OFFICE: 3201 Interstate Avenue, Fargo, ND  58103-8773 (701) 555-1294

Neil W. Webster, Barbara L. Walker, Tomas J. Lopez
SATELLITE OFFICE: 2213 Roosevelt Avenue, Moorhead, MN  56560-9909 (218) 555-1781

stefansen
cohen &
skramstad

**Attorneys at Law**

Gail S. Stefansen, Bernard J. Cohen, Ann D. Skramstad
HOME OFFICE: 3201 Interstate Avenue, Fargo, ND 58103-8773 (701) 555-1294

Neil W. Webster, Barbara L. Walker, Tomas J. Lopez
SATELLITE OFFICE: 2213 Roosevelt Avenue, Moorhead, MN 56560-9909 (218) 555-1781

stefansen
cohen &
skramstad

**Attorneys at Law**

Gail S. Stefansen, Bernard J. Cohen, Ann D. Skramstad
HOME OFFICE: 3201 Interstate Avenue, Fargo, ND  58103-8773 (701) 555-1294

Neil W. Webster, Barbara L. Walker, Tomas J. Lopez
SATELLITE OFFICE: 2213 Roosevelt Avenue, Moorhead, MN  56560-9909 (218) 555-1781

Case 4

95

stefansen, cohen & skramstad

# Interoffice Memo

TO:                                   DATE:

FROM:                                 SUBJECT:

# CASE 5

# WILLS AND PROBATE

| CLIENT'S NAME | ATTORNEY FOR CLIENT |
|---|---|
| Mabel K. Turner<br>1121 Southwood Circle<br>Fargo, ND 58103-7799 | Tomas J. Lopez<br>STEFANSEN, COHEN & SKRAMSTAD<br>3201 Interstate Avenue<br>Fargo, ND 58103-8773<br>(701) 555-1294<br>North Dakota License #436871<br>Office File Number: TJL457-2 |

**CASE SUMMARY**

This case involves the preparation of a Last Will and Testament and a Codicil for Marcus Quentin Turner. Persons must be of legal age in their state (usually 18 or 21) to draw up a will, and a will must be signed in the presence of at least two witnesses (depending on state law), with their names and addresses added. The witnesses must attest to the fact that the testator or testatrix (male or female maker of the will) is of legal age and sound mind when signing the will. This attestation clause is an important part of every will prepared.

When Mr. Turner died, his property was distributed through probate proceedings. Although state laws regarding probate procedure vary considerably, the terminology associated with wills and probate is standard.

**SPECIAL INSTRUCTIONS**

1. Refer to the reference section of your text-workbook for model documents and rules for formatting probate papers.
2. Legal cap is commonly used for keying wills and codicils. Be sure to set your margins 2 to 3 spaces within the ruled lines when using this type of paper.
3. Wills and codicils must be keyed without any misspelling of names or typographical errors. As a precaution against the unauthorized insertions of pages, a will should not be taken apart after it has been stapled.
4. Job #9 is a form letter that is to be sent to all the heirs of Marcus Quentin Turner. Address one letter to each of the six heirs, supplying a current date for each letter.
5. Heirs to the estate of Marcus Quentin Turner are Mabel K. Turner and her children, Jeffrey Donald Turner, Steven Gary Turner, Darrel Martin Turner, Douglas Quentin Turner, and Tricia Kay Turner. All reside with Mabel K. Turner, their mother, at 1121 Southwood Circle, Fargo, ND 58103-7799.

**DOCUMENTS INCLUDED**

1. Last Will and Testament
2. Codicil
3. Letter to Probate Court
4. Letter to Department of Human Services
5. Application for Informal Probate of Will and Appointment of a Personal Representative with Affidavit of Service by Mail
6. Statement of Informal Probate of Will and Appointment of a Personal Representative

## WILLS AND PROBATE TERMINOLOGY

| WORDS | DEFINITIONS |
| --- | --- |
| Administrator | Person appointed by the court to settle the estate of one who died without a will |
| attestation | Act of witnessing the signing of a document and signing it as a witness |
| beneficiary | A person who inherits under a will |
| bequest | A gift by will of personal property or money (as opposed to real estate) |
| Codicil | A supplement or addition to a will |
| conservator | A guardian or preserver of property appointed for a person who cannot legally manage his/her property |
| convey | To transfer title to real property |
| creditor | Person to whom a debt is owed |
| decedent | A person who has died |
| devise | A gift of real property |
| devisee | One who inherits real property (land) |
| distribute in kind | Distribute assets as they exist, rather than converting them to cash |
| domicile | A person's permanent home, legal home, or main residence |
| estate | The interest a person has in property; a person's right or title to property; things left by a deceased person |
| Executor/Executrix | One who represents the decedent in carrying out the terms of a will |
| guardian | Person appointed to care for and manage the person and/or property of a minor or incompetent who cannot legally act for him/herself |
| heir | A person who has a legal right to inherit property if an ancestor dies without leaving a valid will (intestate) |
| intestate | Dying without leaving a valid will |
| personal property | Movable property |
| Personal Representative | One who represents the decedent in carrying out the terms of a will |
| probate | The process of (1) proving before a judicial authority that a will is valid and (2) disbursing |

| WORDS | DEFINITIONS |
|---|---|
| ratify | To confirm a previous act |
| real property | Land and things attached to the land such as buildings |
| residuary estate | That part of the estate remaining after payment of all debts and legacies |
| surety bond | An insurance agreement pledging surety for financial loss caused to another by the failure of the principal (the insured) to perform |
| tangible | Capable of being appraised at an actual or approximate value |
| testament | A will |
| testamentary | Having to do with a will (e.g., testamentary capacity is the mental ability to make a valid will) |
| testate | Leaving a valid will |
| Testator | A male person who makes a will |
| Testatrix | A female person who makes a will |
| therefor | For or in return for that (e.g., ''I have received your invoice for $500 and the check therefor will be mailed immediately) |
| to wit | Namely; that is to say |

Source: Daniel Oran, J.D., *Law Dictionary for Nonlawyers*, 2nd ed. (St. Paul, MN: West Publishing Company, 1985).

stefansen
cohen &
skramstad

**Attorneys at Law**

Gail S. Stefansen, Bernard J. Cohen, Ann D. Skramstad
HOME OFFICE: 3201 Interstate Avenue, Fargo, ND  58103-8773 (701) 555-1294

Neil W. Webster, Barbara L. Walker, Tomas J. Lopez
SATELLITE OFFICE: 2213 Roosevelt Avenue, Moorhead, MN  56560-9909 (218) 555-1781

stefansen
cohen &
skramstad

**Attorneys at Law**

Gail S. Stefansen, Bernard J. Cohen, Ann D. Skramstad
HOME OFFICE: 3201 Interstate Avenue, Fargo, ND  58103-8773 (701) 555-1294

Neil W. Webster, Barbara L. Walker, Tomas J. Lopez
SATELLITE OFFICE: 2213 Roosevelt Avenue, Moorhead, MN  56560-9909 (218) 555-1781

stefansen
cohen &
skramstad

**Attorneys at Law**

Gail S. Stefansen, Bernard J. Cohen, Ann D. Skramstad
HOME OFFICE: 3201 Interstate Avenue, Fargo, ND 58103-8773 (701) 555-1294

Neil W. Webster, Barbara L. Walker, Tomas J. Lopez
SATELLITE OFFICE: 2213 Roosevelt Avenue, Moorhead, MN 56560-9909 (218) 555-1781

stefansen
cohen &
skramstad

Case 5

119

**Attorneys at Law**

Gail S. Stefansen, Bernard J. Cohen, Ann D. Skramstad
HOME OFFICE: 3201 Interstate Avenue, Fargo, ND  58103-8773 (701) 555-1294

Neil W. Webster, Barbara L. Walker, Tomas J. Lopez
SATELLITE OFFICE: 2213 Roosevelt Avenue, Moorhead, MN  56560-9909 (218) 555-1781

stefansen
cohen &
skramstad

**Attorneys at Law**

Gail S. Stefansen, Bernard J. Cohen, Ann D. Skramstad
HOME OFFICE: 3201 Interstate Avenue, Fargo, ND  58103-8773 (701) 555-1294

Neil W. Webster, Barbara L. Walker, Tomas J. Lopez
SATELLITE OFFICE: 2213 Roosevelt Avenue, Moorhead, MN  56560-9909 (218) 555-1781

stefansen
cohen &
skramstad

**Attorneys at Law**

Gail S. Stefansen, Bernard J. Cohen, Ann D. Skramstad
HOME OFFICE: 3201 Interstate Avenue, Fargo, ND 58103-8773 (701) 555-1294

Neil W. Webster, Barbara L. Walker, Tomas J. Lopez
SATELLITE OFFICE: 2213 Roosevelt Avenue, Moorhead, MN 56560-9909 (218) 555-1781

stefansen
cohen &
skramstad

**Attorneys at Law**

Gail S. Stefansen, Bernard J. Cohen, Ann D. Skramstad
HOME OFFICE: 3201 Interstate Avenue, Fargo, ND  58103-8773 (701) 555-1294

Neil W. Webster, Barbara L. Walker, Tomas J. Lopez
SATELLITE OFFICE: 2213 Roosevelt Avenue, Moorhead, MN  56560-9909 (218) 555-1781

stefansen
cohen &
skramstad

**Attorneys at Law**

Gail S. Stefansen, Bernard J. Cohen, Ann D. Skramstad
HOME OFFICE: 3201 Interstate Avenue, Fargo, ND  58103-8773 (701) 555-1294

Neil W. Webster, Barbara L. Walker, Tomas J. Lopez
SATELLITE OFFICE: 2213 Roosevelt Avenue, Moorhead, MN  56560-9909 (218) 555-1781

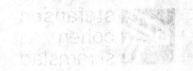

stefansen
cohen &
skramstad

**Attorneys at Law**

Gail S. Stefansen, Bernard J. Cohen, Ann D. Skramstad
HOME OFFICE: 3201 Interstate Avenue, Fargo, ND 58103-8773 (701) 555-1294

Neil W. Webster, Barbara L. Walker, Tomas J. Lopez
SATELLITE OFFICE: 2213 Roosevelt Avenue, Moorhead, MN 56560-9909 (218) 555-1781

stefansen
cohen &
skramstad

**Attorneys at Law**

Gail S. Stefansen, Bernard J. Cohen, Ann D. Skramstad
HOME OFFICE: 3201 Interstate Avenue, Fargo, ND  58103-8773 (701) 555-1294

Neil W. Webster, Barbara L. Walker, Tomas J. Lopez
SATELLITE OFFICE: 2213 Roosevelt Avenue, Moorhead, MN  56560-9909 (218) 555-1781

stefansen
cohen &
skramstad

**Attorneys at Law**

Gail S. Stefansen, Bernard J. Cohen, Ann D. Skramstad
HOME OFFICE: 3201 Interstate Avenue, Fargo, ND  58103-8773 (701) 555-1294

Neil W. Webster, Barbara L. Walker, Tomas J. Lopez
SATELLITE OFFICE: 2213 Roosevelt Avenue, Moorhead, MN  56560-9909 (218) 555-1781

# CASE 6
# PERSONAL INJURY LITIGATION

<table>
<tr><td>

**PLAINTIFF**

Carole M. Baker
519 Second Avenue East
Hawley, MN  56549-5275

**PLAINTIFF'S ATTORNEY**

Gail S. Stefansen
STEFANSEN, COHEN &
  SKRAMSTAD
3201 Interstate Avenue
Fargo, ND  58103-8773
(701) 555-1294
Minnesota License #203892
Office File Number: GS02177-PI

</td><td>

**DEFENDANT**

South Plaza Hardware
1742 Roosevelt Avenue South
Moorhead, MN  56560-2673

**DEFENDANT'S ATTORNEY**

Jennifer P. Gray
TOWERS, GRAY & MOORE
413 East Central Avenue
Moorhead, MN  56560-1776
(218) 555-1987
Minnesota License #273780
Office File Number: P-6738-1

</td></tr>
</table>

**CASE SUMMARY**

This case is a personal injury action wherein the plaintiff claims damages for injuries sustained when she was struck by utility cans falling from a display shelf in a hardware store. The plaintiff claims negligence on the part of the hardware store employee. The case was tried by jury, who awarded the plaintiff less damages than were sued for.

**SPECIAL INSTRUCTIONS**

1. Use this caption for all documents in this case:

```
STATE OF MINNESOTA                    IN DISTRICT COURT

COUNTY OF CLAY                   SEVENTH JUDICIAL DISTRICT


Carole M. Baker,            )      (Personal Injury)
                            )
              Plaintiff,    )      CIVIL NO. _____
                            )
      vs.                   )      NAME OF DOCUMENT
                            )
South Plaza Hardware,       )
                            )
              Defendant.    )
_____)
```

**DOCUMENTS INCLUDED**

1. Memo
2. Summons
3. Complaint
4. Letter to Sheriff
5. Letter to Gail S. Stefansen
6. Answer
7. Interrogatories to Plaintiff
8. Request for Medical Disclosure and Production of Documents with Affidavit of Service by Mail
9. Letter to Jennifer P. Gray
10. Answers to Interrogatories with Affidavit of Service by Mail
11. Letter to Gail S. Stefansen
12. Notice of Taking Deposition
13. Letter to Gail S. Stefansen
14. Certificate of Readiness
15. Subpoena Duces Tecum
16. Special Verdict Form
17. Letter to Judge
18. Order for Judgment
19. Production Test for Case 6—Notice to Take Deposition

**PERSONAL INJURY LITIGATION TERMINOLOGY**

| WORDS | DEFINITIONS |
| --- | --- |
| actual or compensatory damages | Damages directly related to the amount of of the loss |
| affidavit | A written, signed statement of facts sworn to before a notary public |
| allege | To state, assert, charge, or make an allegation |
| answer | Pleading by a defendant in a lawsuit that responds to the charges and demands of the plaintiff |
| appeal | Request to a higher court to review the actions of a lower court in order to correct mistakes or injustices |
| cause of action | The facts that support a valid lawsuit |
| certificate of readiness | Document to the court stating that both sides are ready for trial |
| complaint | First pleading in a lawsuit that states the wrong or harm done to the plaintiff by the defendant and requests help from the court |
| costs and disbursements | Funds paid out on behalf of the client during the course of a lawsuit |
| damages | The plaintiff's claim for money in a legal pleading |
| defendant | Person against whom a legal action is brought |
| deposition | The process of taking a witness's sworn testimony out of court before a notary public (usually all attorneys in the action may attend the deposition and participate in questioning the witness) |

| WORDS | DEFINITIONS |
| --- | --- |
| discovery | The formal and informal exchange of information between sides in a lawsuit (two types of discovery are interrogatories and depositions) |
| exemplary or punitive damages | Money that is awarded by the court to punish the defendant in addition to compensatory damages |
| exhibit | Any object or document that is offered as evidence |
| interrogatories | A set of written questions used in discovery proceedings |
| liability | Legal obligation, responsibility, or debt |
| litigation | A lawsuit |
| motion | Application to the court for a ruling or some other action |
| negotiate | Discuss, arrange, or bargain a settlement of a lawsuit; discuss a compromise to a situation |
| notice | Communication of information by authorized person |
| order | A written command or direction given by the court |
| personal injury litigation | A lawsuit based on negligence |
| plaintiff | Person who brings a lawsuit against another person |
| proximate cause | The real cause of an accident or other injury |
| special verdict | The jury is asked to give its findings on specific questions of fact |
| subpoena duces tecum | Commands a person to appear in court and bring certain documents |
| testimony | Evidence given by a witness under oath |
| verdict | The decision of the jury |

Source: Daniel Oran, J.D., *Law Dictionary for Nonlawyers*, 2nd ed. (St. Paul, MN: West Publishing Company, 1985).

stefansen, cohen & skramstad

# Interoffice Memo

TO:                                      DATE:

FROM:                                    SUBJECT:

stefansen
cohen &
skramstad

**Attorneys at Law**

Gail S. Stefansen, Bernard J. Cohen, Ann D. Skramstad
HOME OFFICE: 3201 Interstate Avenue, Fargo, ND  58103-8773 (701) 555-1294

Neil W. Webster, Barbara L. Walker, Tomas J. Lopez
SATELLITE OFFICE: 2213 Roosevelt Avenue, Moorhead, MN  56560-9909 (218) 555-1781

stefansen
cohen &
skramstad

**Attorneys at Law**

Gail S. Stefansen, Bernard J. Cohen, Ann D. Skramstad
HOME OFFICE: 3201 Interstate Avenue, Fargo, ND  58103-8773 (701) 555-1294

Neil W. Webster, Barbara L. Walker, Tomas J. Lopez
SATELLITE OFFICE: 2213 Roosevelt Avenue, Moorhead, MN  56560-9909 (218) 555-1781

# TOWERS, GRAY & MOORE

413 East Central Avenue, Moorhead, MN  56560-1776

(218) 555-1987

# TOWERS, GRAY & MOORE

413 East Central Avenue, Moorhead, MN   56560-1776

(218) 555-1987

# TOWERS, GRAY & MOORE

413 East Central Avenue, Moorhead, MN   56560-1776

(218) 555-1987

# TOWERS, GRAY & MOORE

413 East Central Avenue, Moorhead, MN   56560-1776

(218) 555-1987

# CASE 7
# RESCISSION AND REVOCATION OF CONTRACT

| PLAINTIFFS | DEFENDANTS |
|---|---|
| Larry G. Hardy<br>Jaime P. Hardy<br>1802 May Lane<br>Fargo, ND  58102-0079 | Gaines Home Sales, Inc.<br>Highway 10 West<br>West Fargo, ND  58078-5565<br>(Fritz Taylor, President)<br><br>Dunn Manufacturing, Inc.<br>820 North Highway 20<br>Grand Forks, ND  58201-8765<br>(William Quinn, President) |
| **PLAINTIFFS' ATTORNEY** | **DEFENDANTS' ATTORNEY** |
| Ann D. Skramstad<br>STEFANSEN, COHEN &<br>   SKRAMSTAD<br>3201 Interstate Avenue<br>Fargo, ND  58103-8773<br>(701) 555-1294<br>North Dakota License #508777<br>Office File Number: ADS96712-90 | Karen Reinhaus<br>REINHAUS & JOHNSON<br>906 42nd Street North<br>Fargo, ND  58102-9876<br>(701) 555-3910<br>North Dakota License #523880<br>Office File Number: 801-420R |

**CASE SUMMARY**

This case involves a purchase agreement for a 28-x-36-foot Rambler-Style Modular Home, Serial #982146890, between Larry G. and Jaime P. Hardy and Gaines Home Sales, Inc. The modular home was delivered to Larry and Jaime Hardy and erected on their lot.

After a period of time, Larry and Jaime Hardy claimed there were many defects in the modular home. They retained counsel and served notice on Gaines Home Sales, Inc. that they were rescinding the purchase contract for the home on the grounds that these defects constituted lack of consideration under the contract on the part of Gaines. Gaines Home Sales, Inc. alleged that the claims should have been addressed to the manufacturer of the modular home, Dunn Manufacturing, Inc.

Larry and Jaime Hardy proceeded to revoke their acceptance of the modular home and initiated a lawsuit against both the seller and the manufacturer of the modular home.

Through negotiations between the attorneys for the parties, a settlement was reached, and the case was dismissed with no further claims by either party.

1. Use this caption on the summons and complaint for this case:

```
        IN THE DISTRICT COURT FOR CASS COUNTY, NORTH DAKOTA


   Larry G. Hardy and            )
   Jaime P. Hardy,               )
                                 )
                 Plaintiffs,     )      CIVIL NO. _____
                                 )
        vs.                      )      NAME OF DOCUMENT
                                 )
   Dunn Manufacturing, Inc., a   )
   Grand Forks, North Dakota,    )
   corporation, and Gaines Home  )
   Sales, Inc., a West Fargo,    )
   North Dakota, corporation,    )
                                 )
                 Defendants.     )
   _____)
```

2. As this case progresses through negotiations, you will key documents prepared by the plaintiffs' attorney and correspondence from both the plaintiffs' attorney and the defendants' attorney.
3. Since Jobs #8 and #9 both contain an admission of service, a form could be prepared and photocopied with information relating to both jobs filled in on the copies. If you are working on word processing equipment, this document could be block copied to a new document.

**DOCUMENTS**
**INCLUDED**

1. Letter to Gaines Home Sales, Inc.
2. Notice of Rescission with Affidavit of Service by Mail
3. Letter to Ann D. Skramstad
4. Letter to Dunn Manufacturing, Inc.
5. Letter to Karen Reinhaus
6. Notice of Revocation of Acceptance of Modular Home
7. Summons and Complaint
8. Admission of Service by Gaines Home Sales, Inc.
9. Admission of Service by Dunn Manufacturing, Inc.
10. Letter to Ann D. Skramstad
11. Letter to Ann D. Skramstad
12. Letter to Karen Reinhaus
13. Letter to Ann D. Skramstad
14. Letter to Karen Reinhaus
15. Letter to Ann D. Skramstad
16. Stipulation of Dismissal
17. Release of All Claims
18. Production Test for Case 7—Stipulation of Dismissal without Prejudice

| WORDS | DEFINITIONS |
|---|---|
| acceptance | Agreeing to an offer and becoming bound by the terms |
| admission of service | An acknowledgment that a document has been received |
| affidavit of service by mail | Sworn statement that a legal paper has been served upon another person in a lawsuit |
| allegation | A statement in a pleading that one side expects to prove |
| apportion | To divide into parts or shares |
| cause of action | The facts that support a valid lawsuit |
| civil action | A lawsuit that is brought to enforce a right or gain payment for a wrong |
| complaint | First pleading in a lawsuit that states the wrong or harm done to the plaintiff by the defendant and requests help from the court |
| consideration | Something of value received or promised to induce (convince) a person to enter a contract |
| contract | Agreement between two or more competent persons |
| counsel | A lawyer for a client |
| count | Each cause of action in the complaint (a complaint may have one or more causes of action or counts) |
| defendant | The person against whom a legal action is brought |
| exhibit | Any object or document that is offered as evidence |
| negotiate | Discuss, arrange, or bargain a settlement of a lawsuit; discuss a compromise to a situation |
| nonconformity | Failure to meet specifications |
| N.D.C.C. | North Dakota Century Code (a series of books containing the statutes adopted by the state of North Dakota) |
| plaintiff | The person who starts a lawsuit against another person |
| prayer clause | Final paragraph of a pleading demanding judgment against the defendant for a specific sum or demanding that the complaint be dismissed |
| pursuant | In accordance with |
| release | The giving up or relinquishing of a claim or a right by the person who has it to the person against whom it might have been enforced |
| rescind | To cancel, annul, or make void |
| revoke | To take back some power or authority; to cancel, annul, or rescind |
| statutes | Laws passed by a legislature |
| stipulation of dismissal with prejudice | Agreement to dismiss an action and bar any future lawsuit on same cause of action |

| WORDS | DEFINITIONS |
|-------|-------------|
| therefor | For or in return for that (e.g, "I have received your invoice for $500 and the check therefor will be mailed immediately") |
| U.C.C. | Uniform Commercial Code (a comprehensive set of laws on every major type of business law that has been adopted by almost every state, in whole or in major part) |
| verification | A form of affidavit executed by the party making the pleading that states that allegations contained in pleading are true |
| warranty | Express or implied guarantee as to the quality, content, or condition of a product sold |

Source: Daniel Oran, J.D., *Law Dictionary for Nonlawyers*, 2nd ed. (St. Paul, MN: West Publishing Company, 1985).

stefansen
cohen &
skramstad

**Attorneys at Law**

Gail S. Stefansen, Bernard J. Cohen, Ann D. Skramstad
HOME OFFICE: 3201 Interstate Avenue, Fargo, ND 58103-8773 (701) 555-1294

Neil W. Webster, Barbara L. Walker, Tomas J. Lopez
SATELLITE OFFICE: 2213 Roosevelt Avenue, Moorhead, MN 56560-9909 (218) 555-1781

stefansen
cohen &
skramstad

**Attorneys at Law**

Gail S. Stefansen, Bernard J. Cohen, Ann D. Skramstad
HOME OFFICE: 3201 Interstate Avenue, Fargo, ND 58103-8773 (701) 555-1294

Neil W. Webster, Barbara L. Walker, Tomas J. Lopez
SATELLITE OFFICE: 2213 Roosevelt Avenue, Moorhead, MN 56560-9909 (218) 555-1781

stefansen
cohen &
skramstad

Case 7

165

**Attorneys at Law**

Gail S. Stefansen, Bernard J. Cohen, Ann D. Skramstad
HOME OFFICE: 3201 Interstate Avenue, Fargo, ND  58103-8773 (701) 555-1294

Neil W. Webster, Barbara L. Walker, Tomas J. Lopez
SATELLITE OFFICE: 2213 Roosevelt Avenue, Moorhead, MN  56560-9909 (218) 555-1781

stefansen
cohen &
skramstad

**Attorneys at Law**

Gail S. Stefansen, Bernard J. Cohen, Ann D. Skramstad
HOME OFFICE: 3201 Interstate Avenue, Fargo, ND  58103-8773 (701) 555-1294

Neil W. Webster, Barbara L. Walker, Tomas J. Lopez
SATELLITE OFFICE: 2213 Roosevelt Avenue, Moorhead, MN  56560-9909 (218) 555-1781

stefansen
cohen &
skramstad

**Attorneys at Law**

Gail S. Stefansen, Bernard J. Cohen, Ann D. Skramstad
HOME OFFICE: 3201 Interstate Avenue, Fargo, ND 58103-8773 (701) 555-1294

Neil W. Webster, Barbara L. Walker, Tomas J. Lopez
SATELLITE OFFICE: 2213 Roosevelt Avenue, Moorhead, MN 56560-9909 (218) 555-1781

# REINHAUS & JOHNSON

906 42nd Street North, Fargo, ND 58102-9876
(701) 555-3910

# REINHAUS & JOHNSON

906 42nd Street North, Fargo, ND 58102-9876
(701) 555-3910

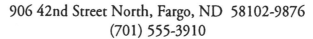

# REINHAUS & JOHNSON

906 42nd Street North, Fargo, ND 58102-9876
(701) 555-3910

# REINHAUS & JOHNSON

906 42nd Street North, Fargo, ND  58102-9876
(701) 555-3910

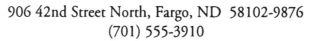

# REINHAUS & JOHNSON

906 42nd Street North, Fargo, ND  58102-9876
(701) 555-3910

# CASE 8
# CORPORATE

| CLIENT | INCORPORATORS |
|---|---|
| Century Park, Inc.<br>4001 Highlake Road<br>Minneapolis, MN 55439-2071 | John J. Brainard<br>2201 Field Avenue<br>St. Paul, MN 55113-9656 |
| **CLIENT'S ATTORNEY**<br>Bernard J. Cohen<br>STEFANSEN, COHEN &<br>SKRAMSTAD<br>3201 Interstate Avenue<br>Fargo, ND 58103-8773<br>(701) 555-1294<br>Minnesota License #491024<br>Office File Number: BJC73041-50 | Nancy S. Smith<br>1511 Belmont Avenue<br>Minneapolis, MN 55439-8424<br><br>Jessica R. Steele<br>4202 Florida Drive<br>Minneapolis, MN 55439-7231 |

**CASE SUMMARY**

A corporation is a legal entity created under the laws of the state in which it is incorporated. A corporation may be public (set up by the government) or private (set up by individuals). It may be set up to carry on a business or to perform almost any legal function either for profit or nonprofit. Corporate law, a specialty in many law firms, involves many different types of documents. It is important for a legal secretary to understand the procedures involved in this form of law. Although corporate law differs from state to state, the terminology and procedures presented in this case are similar in all states. The company that is being incorporated in this case is Century Park, Inc., and it will have general business purposes.

This case will take you through the process of incorporating a business. You will be preparing all the necessary documents to form a corporation and all the necessary correspondence to obtain corporate status in the state where Century Park, Inc. is located.

**SPECIAL INSTRUCTIONS**

1. When preparing a stock certificate for each of the three incorporators, use the following information:

   Certificate #1, John J. Brainard—1000 shares
   Certificate #2, Jessica R. Steele—500 shares
   Certificate #3, Nancy S. Smith—500 shares

2. Date the certificates January 8, 19xx.

**DOCUMENTS INCLUDED**

1. Letter to Secretary of State
2. Articles of Incorporation
3. Letter to Secretary of State
4. Bylaws of Century Park, Inc.
5. Minutes of the First Meeting of Board of Directors
6. Call and Waiver of Notice of First Meeting of Incorporators and Shareholders
7. Minutes of First Meeting of Incorporators and Shareholders
8. Action in Writing by Shareholders
9. Form Letter to Each of the Three Shareholders

10. Three Stock Certificates (Preprinted Forms Provided)
11. Production Test for Case 8—Minutes of First Meeting of Board of Directors

## CORPORATE TERMINOLOGY

| WORDS | DEFINITIONS |
|---|---|
| agenda | A list, outline, or plan of things to be considered or done |
| amortization | Paying off a debt in regular and equal payments; any dividing up of benefits or costs by time periods |
| articles of incorporation | Document setting forth name, place, and purpose of business, among other things (upon approval by the Secretary of State, this document becomes the corporation's charter) |
| blue sky laws | State laws regulating sales of stock and other activities of investment companies to protect the public from fly-by-night or fraudulent stock deals |
| bylaws | Rules and regulations adopted by an organization by which the organization will be governed |
| charter | An organization's official license or authority to function as a corporation |
| consent | Voluntary and active agreement |
| corporation | An organization that is formed under State or Federal law and exists, for legal purposes, as a separate being or artificial person |
| cumulative | Made up of accumulated parts |
| eleemosynary | Charitable corporation (pronounce: el-e-<u>mos</u>-e-nary) |
| entity | A person or legally recognized organization |
| incorporator | One of the persons who formally creates a corporation |
| incumbent | A person who presently holds an office |
| indemnification | Act of insuring that compensation or reimbursement will be made for any loss a person may suffer as a result of acts performed at the request of or on behalf of the indemnifier |
| liquidation | Paying off or settling a debt |
| par value | At face value (e.g., if a $100 bond sells in the bond market for $100, it sells at par) |
| pecuniary | Relating to money |
| plurality | The greatest number |
| proxy | A person who acts for another person, usually to vote in a meeting; the document authorizing a person to vote on behalf of the signer of the document |
| power of attorney | A document authorizing a person to act for the person signing the document |
| quorum | The number of persons who must be present to make the votes and other actions of a group (such as the board) valid |

| WORDS | DEFINITIONS |
|---|---|
| resolution | A decision to do something |
| securities | Stocks, bonds, notes, or other documents that show ownership in a company |
| Securities and Exchange Commission (SEC) | Federal agency that regulates the sale of corporate securities, such as stocks, bonds, notes, or other documents, that show ownership in a coroporation or debt owed by a publicly owned corporation |
| shareholder | One who holds or owns a share in a corporation as a stockholder |
| statute | A law passed by a legislature |
| statutory | Having to do with a statute; created, defined or required by a statute |
| stockholder | An owner of corporate stock |
| subscriber | Person who agrees to purchase initial unissued stock in a corporation |
| subscription rights | The right of existing shareholders to purchase additional shares of stock of the same kind held when new shares are issued by corporation |
| waiver | The voluntary giving up of a right |

Source: Daniel Oran, J.D., *Law Dictionary for Nonlawyers*, 2nd ed. (St. Paul, MN: West Publishing Company, 1985).

stefansen
cohen &
skramstad

**Attorneys at Law**

Gail S. Stefansen, Bernard J. Cohen, Ann D. Skramstad
HOME OFFICE: 3201 Interstate Avenue, Fargo, ND 58103-8773 (701) 555-1294

Neil W. Webster, Barbara L. Walker, Tomas J. Lopez
SATELLITE OFFICE: 2213 Roosevelt Avenue, Moorhead, MN 56560-9909 (218) 555-1781

stefansen
cohen &
skramstad

**Attorneys at Law**

Gail S. Stefansen, Bernard J. Cohen, Ann D. Skramstad
HOME OFFICE: 3201 Interstate Avenue, Fargo, ND  58103-8773 (701) 555-1294

Neil W. Webster, Barbara L. Walker, Tomas J. Lopez
SATELLITE OFFICE: 2213 Roosevelt Avenue, Moorhead, MN  56560-9909 (218) 555-1781

stefansen
cohen &
skramstad

**Attorneys at Law**

Gail S. Stefansen, Bernard J. Cohen, Ann D. Skramstad
HOME OFFICE: 3201 Interstate Avenue, Fargo, ND 58103-8773 (701) 555-1294

Neil W. Webster, Barbara L. Walker, Tomas J. Lopez
SATELLITE OFFICE: 2213 Roosevelt Avenue, Moorhead, MN 56560-9909 (218) 555-1781

stefansen
cohen &
skramstad

**Attorneys at Law**

Gail S. Stefansen, Bernard J. Cohen, Ann D. Skramstad
HOME OFFICE: 3201 Interstate Avenue, Fargo, ND  58103-8773 (701) 555-1294

Neil W. Webster, Barbara L. Walker, Tomas J. Lopez
SATELLITE OFFICE: 2213 Roosevelt Avenue, Moorhead, MN  56560-9909 (218) 555-1781

stefansen
cohen &
skramstad

**Attorneys at Law**

Gail S. Stefansen, Bernard J. Cohen, Ann D. Skramstad
HOME OFFICE: 3201 Interstate Avenue, Fargo, ND 58103-8773 (701) 555-1294

Neil W. Webster, Barbara L. Walker, Tomas J. Lopez
SATELLITE OFFICE: 2213 Roosevelt Avenue, Moorhead, MN 56560-9909 (218) 555-1781

SHARES

NUMBER

This Certifies That

is the owner of

Shares of the Capital Stock of

transferable only on the books of the Corporation by the holder hereof in person or by Attorney upon surrender of this Certificate properly endorsed

IN WITNESS WHEREOF, the said Corporation has caused this Certificate to be signed by its duly authorized officers and its Corporate Seal to be hereunto affixed this _____ day of _____ A.D. 19 _____

SHARES EACH

© GOES 136

CERTIFICATE

№

For _____ Shares

Issued to

Dated _____ 19

FROM WHOM TRANSFERRED

Dated _____ 19

| No. Original Certificate | No. Original Shares | No. of Shares Transferred |
|---|---|---|
| | | |

Received Certificate No. _____ Shares

For

this _____ day of _____ 19

For Value Received,_____ hereby sell, assign and transfer unto_____ _____ Shares of the Capital Stock represented by the within Certificate, and do hereby irrevocably constitute and appoint _____ Attorney to transfer the said Stock on the books of the within named Corporation with full power of substitution in the premises. Dated_____ 19____

In presence of

For Value Received, _____ hereby sell, assign and transfer unto

_____

_____ Shares of the Capital Stock represented by the within Certificate and do hereby irrevocably constitute and appoint

_____ Attorney

to transfer the said Stock on the books of the within named Corporation with full power of substitution in the premises.

Dated _____ 19____

In presence of _____

NOTICE: THE SIGNATURE OF THIS ASSIGNMENT MUST CORRESPOND WITH THE NAME AS WRITTEN UPON THE FACE OF THE CERTIFICATE, IN EVERY PARTICULAR WITHOUT ALTERATION OR ENLARGEMENT OR ANY CHANGE WHATEVER.

CERTIFICATE

SHARES

No.

of the Capital Stock

ISSUED TO

DATE

NUMBER

SHARES

This Certifies that

is the owner of

Shares of the Capital Stock of

transferable only on the books of the Corporation by the holder hereof in person or by Attorney upon surrender of this Certificate properly endorsed

IN WITNESS WHEREOF, the said Corporation has caused this Certificate to be signed by its duly authorized officers and its Corporate Seal to be hereunto affixed this _____ day of _____ A.D. 19____

SHARES

EACH

© GOES 136

CERTIFICATE

No.

For _____ Shares

Issued to _____

Dated _____ 19____

FROM WHOM TRANSFERRED

Dated _____ 19____

| No. ORIGINAL CERTIFICATE | No. ORIGINAL SHARES | No. OF SHARES TRANSFERRED |
|---|---|---|
| | | |

Received CERTIFICATE No. _____

For _____ Shares

this _____ day of _____ 19____

For Value Received, _____ hereby sell, assign and transfer unto _____

_____ Shares of the Capital Stock represented by the within Certificate, and do hereby irrevocably constitute and appoint _____ Attorney to transfer the said Stock on the books of the within named Corporation with full power of substitution in the premises.

Dated _____ 19___

In presence of _____

CERTIFICATE

SHARES

of the
Capital Stock

ISSUED TO

DATE

# CASE 9
# DISSOLUTION OF MARRIAGE

| PLAINTIFF | DEFENDANT |
|---|---|
| Michi E. Robinson<br>7186 Roadway Drive<br>West Fargo, ND  58102-4774 | Brian J. Robinson<br>15622 Broadway<br>Fargo, ND  58103-3018 |
| **PLAINTIFF'S ATTORNEY** | **DEFENDANT'S ATTORNEY** |
| Neil W. Webster<br>STEFANSEN, COHEN &<br>   SKRAMSTAD<br>3201 Interstate Avenue<br>Fargo, ND  58103-8773<br>(701) 555-1294<br>North Dakota License #508912<br>Office File Number: NWW2013-90 | Robert M. Sanders<br>SANDERS & SANDERS<br>11 South 22nd Avenue<br>West Fargo, ND  58078-8078<br>(701) 555-2210<br>North Dakota License #761822<br>Office File Number: 76823D |

**CASE SUMMARY**

This is a divorce action venued in the District Court for Cass County, North Dakota. The parties have agreed to an amicable divorce action whereby the plaintiff and defendant each wish to seek a divorce. They will enter into a property settlement agreement and proceed to a judgment and decree of divorce without a trial.

**SPECIAL INSTRUCTIONS**

1.  Use this caption on all documents in this case:

```
        IN THE DISTRICT COURT FOR CASS COUNTY, NORTH DAKOTA


Michi E. Robinson,            )
                              )
              Plaintiff,      )    CIVIL NO. _____
                              )
       vs.                    )    NAME OF DOCUMENT
                              )
Brian J. Robinson,            )
                              )
              Defendant.      )
_____)
```

2. Use these signature blocks on the documents in this case depending on which firm is preparing document:

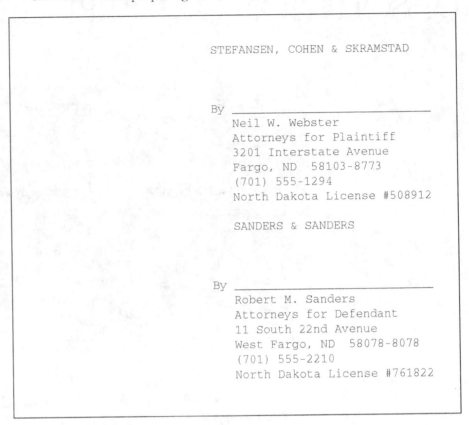

```
                        STEFANSEN, COHEN & SKRAMSTAD



                    By _____
                        Neil W. Webster
                        Attorneys for Plaintiff
                        3201 Interstate Avenue
                        Fargo, ND  58103-8773
                        (701) 555-1294
                        North Dakota License #508912

                        SANDERS & SANDERS



                    By _____
                        Robert M. Sanders
                        Attorneys for Defendant
                        11 South 22nd Avenue
                        West Fargo, ND  58078-8078
                        (701) 555-2210
                        North Dakota License #761822
```

**DOCUMENTS INCLUDED**

1. Summons and Complaint
2. Admission of Service
3. Property Settlement Agreement
4. Findings of Fact, Conclusions of Law, and Order for Judgment
5. Judgment and Decree of Divorce
6. Letter to Defendant's Attorney
7. Notice of Entry of Judgment
8. Affidavit of Service By Mail
9. Production Test for Case 9—Notice of Entry of Judgment

**DISSOLUTION OF MARRIAGE TERMINOLOGY**

| WORDS | DEFINITIONS |
|---|---|
| affiant | A person who executes an affidavit |
| affidavit | A written, signed statement of facts sworn to before a notary public |
| alimony | Court-ordered payments from one divorced spouse to the other for ongoing personal support |
| allege | To state, assert, charge, or make an allegation |
| amicable | On friendly terms; a lawsuit started by agreement of the two sides |
| caption | The title of a court document that includes the venue of the case and the names of the parties |

| WORDS | DEFINITIONS |
|---|---|
| compliance | Acting in a way that does not violate a law or agreement |
| complaint | First pleading in a lawsuit that states the wrong or harm done to the plaintiff by the defendant and that requests help from the court |
| conveyance | The transfer of title to property |
| decree | The order of a Court |
| default | Failure to perform a task or fulfill an obligation |
| dissolution | Ending or breaking up |
| equitable | Just, fair, and right for a particular situation |
| equity | Fairness in a particular situation; a court's power to do justice when specific laws do not cover the situation |
| irreconcilable differences | Grounds for divorce in a no-fault divorce state |
| issue of a marriage | Children born to the parties of a marriage |
| judgment | The official decision of a court of law |
| pending | As yet undecided; begun but not finished |
| petitioner (plaintiff) | A person who initiates a lawsuit against another person through a petition |
| pleadings | Those documents containing allegations in a legal action |
| prayer | Request; that part of a legal pleading such as a complaint or petition that asks for relief |
| premise | A proposition upon which an argument is based or from which a conclusion is drawn |
| proceedings | A case in court, its orderly progression, or its recorded history |
| relief | The help given by a court to a person who brings a lawsuit (e.g., the relief asked for might be the return of property, enforcement of a contract, or payment of money) |
| respondent (defendant) | The person against whom a lawsuit is brought through a petition |
| stipulation | An agreement between lawyers of opposite sides of a lawsuit (it is often in writing and concerns facts that need no proof) |
| subsist | To exist or continue to exist |
| summons | A document issued in the name of the court notifying the defendant that an action has been started against him/her and requiring the defendant to appear in the action and/or answer the complaint at the risk of the plaintiff being granted the judgment demanded by default |
| to wit | That is to say; namely |

| WORDS | DEFINITIONS |
|---|---|
| venue | The local area where a case may be tried |
| verification | A form of affidavit executed by the party making the pleading that states that allegations contained in the pleading are true |
| waive | Give up, renounce, or disclaim a privilege, right, or benefit with full knowledge of what one is doing |

Source: Daniel Oran, J.D., *Law Dictionary for Nonlawyers*, 2nd ed. (St. Paul, MN: West Publishing Company, 1985).

stefansen
cohen &
skramstad

**Attorneys at Law**

Gail S. Stefansen, Bernard J. Cohen, Ann D. Skramstad
HOME OFFICE: 3201 Interstate Avenue, Fargo, ND 58103-8773 (701) 555-1294

Neil W. Webster, Barbara L. Walker, Tomas J. Lopez
SATELLITE OFFICE: 2213 Roosevelt Avenue, Moorhead, MN 56560-9909 (218) 555-1781

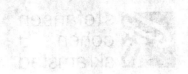

# CASE 10
# MORTGAGE FORECLOSURE

| PLAINTIFF | DEFENDANTS |
|---|---|
| First Northwestern Bank & Trust Co. 81 Main Avenue Fargo, ND 58102-9977 | Ryan D. Whitley Darcy A. Whitley 1316 Ninth Avenue North Fargo, ND 58102-5800 |
| **PLAINTIFF'S ATTORNEY** | **DEFENDANTS' ATTORNEY** |
| Ann D. Skramstad STEFANSEN, COHEN & SKRAMSTAD 3201 Interstate Avenue Fargo, ND 58103-8773 (701) 555-1294 North Dakota License #508777 Office File Number: ADS2379-10 | None on record since defendants never made an appearance in this case |

**CASE SUMMARY**

This mortgage foreclosure action was initiated by the lending institution because the defendants defaulted on the mortgage payments for their home. Because of the default, the bank has taken possession of the home and has proceeded to have the home sold at a Sheriff's sale to satisfy the judgment.

Because of the length of the foreclosure process, some of the pertinent legal documents to this action have been omitted. The cover letters filing and serving these documents have been included, however, so that you may see their proper sequence in this action.

**SPECIAL INSTRUCTIONS**

1. Use this caption for documents in this action:

```
IN DISTRICT COURT, COUNTY OF CASS, STATE OF NORTH DAKOTA


First Northwestern Bank      )
& Trust Co., a Fargo, North  )
Dakota, corporation,         )
                             )
             Plaintiff       )      CIVIL NO. 90-214
                             )
      vs.                    )      NAME OF DOCUMENT
                             )
Ryan D. Whitley and          )
Darcy A. Whitley,            )
                             )
             Defendants.     )
_____)
```

2. Other officials who will sign documents and correspondence in this case and to whom you will address correspondence include Mr. Abel Jackson, Cass County Sheriff, Cass County Courthouse, 1307 Larimer Square, Fargo, ND 58103-6400; Ms. Adriane Simmons, Clerk of District Court, Cass County Courthouse, 1307 Larimer Square, Fargo, ND 58103-6400; and Ms. Rita A. Stolberg, Register of Deeds, Cass County Courthouse, 1307 Larimer Square, Fargo, ND 58103-6400.

3. The property that is the basis of this lawsuit is described as follows:

Lot Fourteen (14) in Block Nine (9), Morningside Addition to the City of Fargo, County of Cass, State of North Dakota; according to the certified plat thereof on file and of record in the Office of the Register of Deeds in and for said County and State.

**DOCUMENTS INCLUDED**

1. Notice of Intention to Foreclose
2. Summons and Complaint
3. Letter to Sheriff Jackson
4. Sheriff's Return
5. Letter to Clerk of District Court
6. Letter to Clerk of District Court Filing Default Judgment Papers
7. Writ of Special Execution with Judgment and Decree
8. Letter to Clerk of District Court
9. Notice of Foreclosure Sale under Special Execution
10. Motion for Order Confirming Sale on Foreclosure
11. Order Confirming Sale on Foreclosure
12. Sheriff's Certificate of Sale on Foreclosure
13. Letter to Sheriff Jackson
14. Sheriff's Deed
15. Letter to Register of Deeds
16. Production Test for Case 10—Affidavit of Default

**MORTGAGE FORECLOSURE TERMINOLOGY**

| WORDS | DEFINITIONS |
|---|---|
| abstract of title | A condensed history of the ownership of a piece of land |
| affiant | A person who makes an affidavit |
| affidavit | A written statement, usually about the truth of a set of facts, sworn to before a person officially permitted by law to administer an oath |
| certificate of sale | Evidence that a person was the successful bidder of foreclosed property and, upon payment of the bid amount, is entitled to receive title to the property |
| decree | A judgment of a court that announces the legal consequences of the facts found in a case and orders that the Court's decision be carried out |
| default | A failure to perform a legal duty, observe a promise, fulfill an obligation, or pay a debt that is due |
| execution | The process of an official carrying out a Court's order or judgment |

| WORDS | DEFINITIONS |
|---|---|
| exhibit | Any object or document offered as evidence or any document attached to a pleading, affidavit, or other formal paper |
| foreclosure | A proceeding whereby the mortgagee (lender) obtains the right to sell the mortgaged property because the mortgagor (owner) has defaulted in the payment of the mortgage loan |
| lien | A claim, charge, or liability against property that is allowed by law |
| merits | The central issues of a claim or a defense |
| mortgage | Document by which owner pledges real property as security for a loan |
| motion | A request to the Court for a ruling or some other action |
| order | A written command or direction of the Court |
| process | Any means used by the court to acquire jurisdiction over a person or property |
| promissory note | A written promise to pay a certain sum of money by a certain time |
| Register of Deeds | An official who maintains public records regarding the official ownership of property |
| return of service | Statement by the Sheriff giving the name of the person served, the date, the place, and the manner of service of a document or an explanation of why the service could not be completed (similar to an affidavit of service) |
| Sheriff | The chief law officer of a county who, with the help of deputies, is in charge of serving process, calling jurors, executing judgments, orders, and writs, keeping the peace, operating the county jail, etc. |
| Sheriff's deed | A document giving ownership rights in property at a Sheriff's sale |
| Sheriff's sale | A court-ordered sale of property by the Sheriff to pay a judgment, mortgage, or other lien |
| writ | A Court order to a Sheriff or other officer authorizing the Sheriff or officer to perform certain actions |

Source: Daniel Oran, J.D., *Law Dictionary for Nonlawyers*, 2nd ed. (St. Paul, MN: West Publishing Company, 1985).

stefansen
cohen &
skramstad

**Attorneys at Law**

Gail S. Stefansen, Bernard J. Cohen, Ann D. Skramstad
HOME OFFICE: 3201 Interstate Avenue, Fargo, ND  58103-8773 (701) 555-1294

Neil W. Webster, Barbara L. Walker, Tomas J. Lopez
SATELLITE OFFICE: 2213 Roosevelt Avenue, Moorhead, MN  56560-9909 (218) 555-1781

stefansen
cohen &
skramstad

**Attorneys at Law**

Gail S. Stefansen, Bernard J. Cohen, Ann D. Skramstad
HOME OFFICE: 3201 Interstate Avenue, Fargo, ND 58103-8773 (701) 555-1294

Neil W. Webster, Barbara L. Walker, Tomas J. Lopez
SATELLITE OFFICE: 2213 Roosevelt Avenue, Moorhead, MN 56560-9909 (218) 555-1781

stefansen
cohen &
skramstad

**Attorneys at Law**

Gail S. Stefansen, Bernard J. Cohen, Ann D. Skramstad
HOME OFFICE: 3201 Interstate Avenue, Fargo, ND 58103-8773 (701) 555-1294

Neil W. Webster, Barbara L. Walker, Tomas J. Lopez
SATELLITE OFFICE: 2213 Roosevelt Avenue, Moorhead, MN 56560-9909 (218) 555-1781

stefansen
cohen &
skramstad

**Attorneys at Law**

Gail S. Stefansen, Bernard J. Cohen, Ann D. Skramstad
HOME OFFICE: 3201 Interstate Avenue, Fargo, ND 58103-8773 (701) 555-1294

Neil W. Webster, Barbara L. Walker, Tomas J. Lopez
SATELLITE OFFICE: 2213 Roosevelt Avenue, Moorhead, MN 56560-9909 (218) 555-1781

stefansen
cohen &
skramstad

**Attorneys at Law**

Gail S. Stefansen, Bernard J. Cohen, Ann D. Skramstad
HOME OFFICE: 3201 Interstate Avenue, Fargo, ND  58103-8773 (701) 555-1294

Neil W. Webster, Barbara L. Walker, Tomas J. Lopez
SATELLITE OFFICE: 2213 Roosevelt Avenue, Moorhead, MN  56560-9909 (218) 555-1781

## Attorneys at Law

Gail S. Stefansen, Bernard J. Cohen, Ann D. Skramstad
HOME OFFICE: 3201 Interstate Avenue, Fargo, ND  58103-8773 (701) 555-1294

Neil W. Webster, Barbara L. Walker, Tomas J. Lopez
SATELLITE OFFICE: 2213 Roosevelt Avenue, Moorhead, MN  56560-9909 (218) 555-1781

# INDEX

Verification clause, 16
Versus (vs., v), 32
Vis a vis, 32
Voir dire, 32

## W

Waive, 204

Waiver, 75
Warranty, 160
Warranty deed, 75
Wills and probate (Case 5), 99–138
Writ, 209